The Re-Enligntenment

A spiritual handbook

Carole and David McEntee-Taylor

*"To create the future we desire we need a spiritual language;
we must speak from the heart and in the language of the
soul—a language of trust, faith and higher values,
of inner growth, love and listening"*

Brahma Kumaris World Spiritual University

FANTINE PRESS

First published in 2007
by
FANTINE PRESS
The Coach House, Stansted Hall
Stansted, Essex CM24 8UD

British Library CIP Data:
A catalogue record of this book is
available from the British Library

ISBN   978 1 901958 12 6

Printed in England by Booksprint

Contents

Preface—A Blueprint for Inclusion   5

1	Introduction	7
2	Why Are We Here?	17
3	Is There Life After Death?	25
4	Is There a God?	37
5	Evolution	45
6	Meditation	52
7	Mediumship	64
8	Questions Asked About Mediums and Readings	75
9	Questions Asked About Spirituality In General	86
10	Healing	101
11	The Principles	115
12	Spiritual Centres	122
13	The End of the Beginning	129
14	Appendix—Spirit Writings	134
15	Bibliography	147

A Blueprint for Inclusion

THE world we currently live in is characterised by multiple interest groups with diverse political, social and religious views. This plurality of cultures leads to conflict, discrimination and destabilisation and ultimately to wars, aided by those whose sole aim is to accelerate this process. Add to this the growing climatic problems and the increasing gap between those who have more than enough and those who are starving and the world seems a very unstable place. The majority of the world's populations not only feel powerless to prevent this, but find it hard to accept the contradictory explanations given by religions, Spiritualism, politics and science.

Despite popular belief, religion, Spiritualism, politics and science all have something in common. This common ground that we all share—whatever our beliefs and cultural background—is our morality. Faith, ethics, the common good—all these describe the shared values that make up our moral view of life and what we consider acceptable behaviour. Another word for this moral identity that we all share is spirituality. Thus spirituality is already a part of all our lives even if we think it isn't.

We believe it is possible to build on this common ground that we all share and establish a world society that uses a non-sectarian spiritual framework to provide the 'glue' that binds us all together. That sounds really complicated but it just means that all societies are held together by something. At present it is by a form of national identity. The elements of this national identity that hold together our society include patriotism, shared history, geographical territory, shared values and culture and a perception that we share certain traits and characteristics that make us different from those citizens of other nations. The problem with some of these things that make up national identity is that they can be used in such a way that they either exclude minorities within the society or demonise other nations. For people to feel part of a group someone has to be on the outside. There are numerous examples in recent history of charismatic leaders vilifying a group either within their society or outside as a way of creating a national identity. Nationalism always has the potential to lead to exclusion and wars.

We believe that it is time to move beyond this narrow form of identity with all its dangers and genuinely see ourselves as citizens of the world. Politically we all inhabit one planet, scientifically we all have to work together to stop the destruction of that one planet and religions and spiritualism tell us that we are all one. To build on this common ground we need to change our perceptions of the world and where better to start than with the most fundamental question of all: Why are we here?

Whatever beliefs we have grown up with, whether we have a religious, scientific or totally agnostic background, we have all at some point asked ourselves this question.

Religions, Spiritualism, politics and science have all provided us with competing explanations but have they provided any real proof? Furthermore, the world as we currently know it is a result of those competing explanations. Its time we looked at another explanation—one that is built on the common ground that religion, spiritualism, science and politics share. This common ground is spirituality.

Chapter 1

Introduction

"The mystics speak in a hundred different ways, but if God is one and the Way is one, how could their meaning be other than one? What appears in different disguises is one essence. A variety of expression, but the same meaning."

Jalal al-Din Rumi
Sufi Sage

WE will begin by looking briefly at how our relationship with religion has changed over time. Why do so few people now go to church or feel that the teachings or messages of the major religions have no relevance for them?

There are several reasons for this. Religions are based on the teachings of people who lived a long time ago. The books based on these teachings were written at a certain time in history and were written in the language of the day. It can be difficult to read something that was written many centuries ago and even more difficult to translate it into modern language. However hard we try to avoid using our 21st century understandings and values some of this is bound to creep into our interpretations. If you add to this the problems of translating from one language to another it is easy to see why we find many religious teachings incompatible with modern life.

The writers of the time could only interpret these teachings in terms that fitted in with their understanding of life at that time. They were often written during periods of considerable upheaval or in times of war. At these times, when it was normal for religious beliefs to provide people with their identity, the same problems that we now experience with nationalism occurred, where "to belong" we have to demonise and exclude "the others."

The teachings were also written within the culture that prevailed at that time. This explains the attitude both Christianity and Islam have towards women. This is not a criticism of either except to say that religions, like everything else, need to change and adapt with time to take into account changes in culture and society and the way in which society views things. Nobody would argue now that slavery is right, yet at the time slavery existed it was considered perfectly acceptable, because that was the way people thought at the time.

Religions are losing their significant place in many of our lives because we have changed and they have not. Many of their teachings seem at odds with the culture and society in which we live. We are, for the most part, better educated and we have learned to question the beliefs that our ancestors took for granted.

What do most religions believe?

Broadly speaking most religions believe that we are one, that there is life after death, that we are responsible for our actions, that we can talk to God through prayer and that we should help each other.

Is Spiritualism a religion?

Spiritualism has always had a bad press. Whether we look at the "witch" hunts in the past or the current fad for treating it as entertainment, the message is clear—spiritualism is dangerous, foolish, subversive, exploitative or just plain loony. But, if it is all these things, why do 67% of the population believe there is some element of truth in its teachings?

Spiritualism has a structure that most world faiths would recognise. It has creeds and codes of conduct, churches, ministers and presidents, officers and committees. Spiritualist gatherings often follow the form of religious services. These include singing, readings, sermons and addresses and money and charity collections. It provides a "family" or comfort and support network for those in need. It also fulfils other "religious" criteria. These include prayer groups, social functions and charity work. Other similarities include the use of music, bells, incense and candles as a part of their rituals.

So what do the majority of Spiritualists believe?

Broadly speaking, Spiritualists believe that we are all spirit, that we are all one, that there is life after life, that we can talk to God/the Great Mind/Spirit through prayer and by means of simple conversation, and that we are responsible for our actions.

What is the difference between Spiritualism and religion?

The answer to that is actually very little. The two main differences between Spiritualism and all other world religions is firstly, the interpretation. Secondly, unlike religions, Spiritualism seeks to provide not only the answers but the proof as well through mediumship.

Spiritualism, like religion, is also interpreted in many different ways. Sometimes it seems that there are almost as many interpretations as there are people. Or are there? All interpretations of Spiritualism are based on the concept of pure unconditional love for every living being. But surely this is the same message the various religions have been trying to promote for centuries? Equally, all the world's "holy" books refer to life after death, healing, trance and mediumship at some point and in addition many talk of reincarnation. With all this common ground it is strange that some religions see Spiritualism as a threat. Aren't we all saying the same thing? The message is simple whether we call it religion or Spiritualism so why complicate it?

What else do religions and Spiritualism have in common?

It seems Spiritualism like religion can never be all things to all people. Both are surrounded by external and internal problems. We all hear stories of churches and spiritual centres closing doors to people of different cultures or beliefs and even, sadly, to those whose appearance is different—perhaps due to disfigurement or

9

accident. We also hear of church committees, run by an elite or clique who seem to have lost their way, are stuck in the past or are just frightened by change.

But is it religion and Spiritualism that are the problem? Unfortunately, because it is open to interpretation, the message has been and still is, frequently manipulated by self-interest, fanaticism, politics, media hype and scepticism. And this is one of the reasons why both religion and Spiritualism are failing the very people they claim to be helping. If we truly believe that God/Allah/the Great Spirit is great, how can we believe that He/She would really tell people to act in this way or to interpret the message in this way? This is just our interpretation of religion and Spiritualism.

A further and more fundamental problem with both Spiritualism and religions is that they do not seem to offer satisfactory answers to our questions. One aim of this book is to address this and to pass on the knowledge that we have. We have tried to cover as many of the most frequently asked questions as we can in the space allowed and if you think about the answers they are all logical and they are all simple.

Finally, both "religion" and "Spiritualism" have particular connotations from which it is very difficult to separate them. It's a bit like the word "handicapped." We no longer use that word because we consider it offensive. There are many narrow interpretations of the message that exclude and in some cases demonise others and these are also offensive. The teachings of religion and Spiritualism have also been deliberately misinterpreted and used to justify atrocities and acts of terrorism. Sadly, these deliberate misinterpretations have led to the indoctrination of many young vulnerable people. Religions, like Spiritualism, were born of love and light. The message of them all is unconditional love for all living beings. There is no place in a concept of unconditional love for hate and murder. They are diametrically opposed. For us to change our world we need to move beyond this. We are therefore proposing that we find the common ground between Spiritualism and religion and take the one word they all use and start again.

"We may distinguish two types of knowledge. There is religious knowledge, which consists of rational theories about God. And there is spiritual or intuitive knowledge, which arises from personal encounters with God. As you acquire spiritual knowledge, you discard religious knowledge."

Junayd: Tawhid 2—Sufi Mysticism

All religions and Spiritualism talk of spirituality. They all work in the light and they all preach love. Let us concentrate on spirituality and see how this common ground is also shared by politics and science.

So—could spirituality become a political movement?

What a novelty—spirituality involved in politics! But why not? We are not talking about religion or Spiritualism as they are currently understood. As previously mentioned religions are culturally and historically specific. In other words they are based in a historical and cultural world that was very different from the world in which we live today where Spiritualism has been turned into an item of entertainment. We need to start again.

We need genuinely to separate religions from politics across the globe and replace them with non-sectarian spirituality. Increasing secularism and the lack of a convincing meaningful spiritual base have led not only to us evolving into a species that sees greed and selfishness as a virtue; they have also bred fanaticism and extremism. In an attempt to counteract the growing secularism there are people who have attempted to introduce a narrow interpretation of the message back into politics and society. This can be seen in all areas of the globe. We can also see that neither religious beliefs nor secularism are sufficient on their own.

Historically we have staggered from one extreme view, when only religious beliefs provided the world with its meaning and identity (before the Enlightenment), to another when only science provided the world with its meaning and identity (after the Enlightenment). As we have now covered both extremes it is time to come back to the middle and find the balance between secularism and spirituality. Both are needed if we are to tackle the problems we see around us. It is now time for the Re-Enlightenment. The Re-Enlightenment builds on the common ground between religions, Spiritualism, politics and science and offers a new message of inclusion to all citizens of the world.

Rational people (those who lean towards scientific explanations) would choose to end poverty and suffering, would choose world peace over war, would choose to ensure there were sufficient resources for all and would choose to ensure there was legal and political equality for all. Religions and Spiritualism would also choose these things. Those politicians who genuinely work for the common good would also choose all those things. Although there may be disagreements over what constitutes "the common good" most people would agree that peace and sufficiency are a reasonable place to start.

This collective spirituality is the common ground between secularism and religion and it is up to us to build on it. Of course this means re-evaluating our way of life and a fundamental shift in the way we think. It means saying, "I choose to make the world a better place to live." Or perhaps you are happy with the way things are?

Where does science fit in with this concept of a new world?

"Science without religion is lame, religion without science is blind."
Albert Einstein (1879–1955)

Finally, let's take a brief look at science. Since the Enlightenment science and religion have been in competition. As we have just said it seems you cannot believe in both because if one is true then the other must be a lie. But is this really true? Science has provided us with some of the most exciting discoveries and advances in all manner of fields. Science has given us the world as we know it today. It is science to which we will turn to find solutions to some of our most pressing environmental concerns and it is science to which we will turn for advances in medicine that will prevent many of our most serious diseases.

"Science is the study of all that exists, with the purpose of understanding the great artisan who created all that exists. The more closely we study his creation, the deeper our knowledge of him will become. The method of study is to infer deeper truths from what we can observe—to infer the unknown from the known. Its tool is reason. Thus we are obliged to study all that exists by means of intellectual reasoning. It follows that science is the most perfect form of study, since intellectual reasoning is the highest human faculty."

Ibn Rushd: Kitab Fasl al-Maqal—Islamic Philosophy

The gap between science and spirituality is not as wide as it first appears. Francis Collins, the director of the US National Human Genome Research Institute claims that scientific discoveries, far from negating the existence of a creator, actually make it easier to believe that there is a rational basis for a belief in a creator.

"When you have for the first time in front of you this 3.1 billion-letter instruction book that conveys all kinds of information and all kinds of mystery about humankind, you can't survey that going through page after page without a sense of awe. I can't help but look at those pages and have a vague sense that this is giving me a glimpse of God's mind." (Francis Collins 2006)

Furthermore, for society really to advance it has long been accepted that ethical considerations must be part of science. The majority of scientists would agree with this.

Ethical considerations are derived from the shared values of the cultures in which we live and are already hotly debated every time a new scientific discovery is made public. They are, in reality, spiritual concerns about the uses to which new discoveries may be put.

However, the diversity of cultures throughout the world makes it difficult to find a common consensus. For instance: many countries consider boys to be more important than girls. There are many reasons for this: some are based on traditional cultural and religious grounds; others on economic grounds. Now that science is in a position to control the ratio of male to

13

female births there is real concern about how this will be used, and many ethical questions have been raised.

If the world came to share one spiritual framework, one moral identity, ethical questions would be much easier to resolve. This would benefit science because the great discoveries that are made with the intention of helping humankind could not be hijacked by self-interested groups who wish to use the advances for their own narrow ends. The world would benefit from scientific advances, safe in the knowledge that as ethical considerations were already embedded within a shared world culture to which everyone subscribed, no-one would be at risk of exploitation.

So is spirituality a way of life?

Yes. If we believe the words and writings of the spiritual messengers across the centuries—then the one constant theme that runs throughout is love and healing and working to improve the life of humanity. Science too maintains that the wellbeing of humanity is its prime motivation. It just does it in a non-religious way. Politics are the means by which the major decisions that affect our lives are made and most politicians also work to improve the lives of the people they represent. Therefore, as we are all already working individually for the good of humanity, there is nothing to stop us all collectively developing a spiritual framework to which we can all subscribe. The common ground is there—the rest (as they say) is mere detail! And where better to start looking at these details than with Chapter 2. Chapters 2 and 3 begin by looking at the basic questions of who we are, where we come from and why we are here. These are not secrets and we believe everybody has a right to know the answers. If we change our perceptions of why we are here we will begin to see our world differently. If we think differently our behaviour will also change because how we act is closely related to how we think. However, in order to change our perceptions we also need to know the answers to the two questions that are covered in Chapters 4 and 5: is there life after death and is there a God? Although these questions may seem quite separate they are in fact closely linked.

This is essentially the theoretical part of the book—the part that sets out the theory our framework is based on. The following chapters show you how the theory translates into practice and how religion, science and politics are already using these practical aspects of our spiritual framework. They also explain how you can use these practical aspects to improve your life and the lives of those around you and how you can find out the answers for yourselves.

Chapter 6 explains what happens when we meditate, shows us how to meditate safely and points out the dangers of meditating and communicating with spirit without using protection. Our spiritual protection is a white light that we all have and are able to use when we know how. It is very simple and prevents many problems that arise from communicating with spirit without first knowing what we are doing. It finishes by looking at how the majority of religions, science and politics are already using meditation.

Two chapters on mediumship follow. The first describes the various types of mediumship and the difference between them. Many people go to see a medium and are disappointed because they have chosen a spiritual medium when they are looking for clairvoyance and vice versa. It also explains how you can get the most out of your visit. The second of these two chapters aims to answer some of the most frequently asked questions about mediums and readings. This is followed by a chapter which covers the more general questions about spiritual philosophy and explores some of the myths surrounding spirit, including what happens when we are unfortunate enough to miscarry or when someone we love commits suicide.

Chapter 10 examines spiritual healing. We start by looking at exactly what spiritual healing is. We then examine some of the myths surrounding spiritual healing and answer some of the most frequently asked questions. We explain how anyone can send absent healing and show you how you can give "contact" healing to yourself, your friends and family. It finishes by looking at the scientific experiments carried out on healing and the political and social benefits of healing for the wider community and yourself.

Theoretical frameworks are based on principles and Chapter 11 lays out the seven principles on which this spiritual framework is based. In Chapter 12 we explain how to set up your own spiritual centre and give you some contact details of organisations that you might find useful.

The final chapter explains how the seemingly diverse threads of the book all knit together and reiterates the common ground which science, politics, religion and Spiritualism share. It is followed by an appendix of spiritual writing.

We finish by asking if you are satisfied with your world or whether you are brave enough to say, "I choose to make the world a better place!"

Chapter 2

Why Are We Here?

"He who faultlessly acts the drama of life that God has given him to play, knows what is to be done and what is to be endured."
Clement of Alexandria
Christian Mystic

"Remember the whole thing is just a play and the Lord has assigned you a part."
Sai Baba
Hindu Guru

"Certainty is the enemy of truth because those who are certain no longer ask questions."
Spirit in meditation

HAVING said that one of the problems with science, politics, religions and spiritualism is that they don't provide satisfactory answers to our questions, we thought we would begin by answering the most basic question of all: Why are we here?—or, put another way—what is the purpose of life?

First of all, it would be impossible for us to answer this question completely in the space we have. All we are doing is giving you a brief idea. Secondly, this is meant to be an introduction to spiritual philosophy and as such we will concentrate on the basics. Finally, nobody here has all the answers. We all have some answers and some people may have more answers than others. But the main point of this book is to help you to open your mind. We don't expect you to take our word for it. But by teaching you how to meditate safely and by debunking some of the myths and hocus-pocus surrounding spirituality you can speak to spirit yourself and find out the answers for yourself. It is very easy to sit and read someone else's view of life but much more satisfying to find out for yourself. Truth and belief are very personal things and are, from a purely physical, earthly point of view, a result of our education and life experiences so far. So, when you have read this book, investigate for yourself, read other explanations and then decide for yourself.

Although the question is "why are we here?" to answer that we need to look first at what we are and where we come from. (No, we are not about to tell you we are aliens!) It's just that what we are and where we come from provides some background which helps to explain the all-important "why are we here?' Although these are separate questions they do overlap and are interconnected. This means that some of the answers also overlap and are also interconnected. However, we will start by trying to isolate and answer the first question:

What are we?

Science tells us that physically we are a collection of cells and DNA that are unique and individual to us. Interestingly enough it is a scientific fact that we all stem from the same gene pool. It seems no two people have exactly the same collection of cells or exactly the same DNA. Our genetic makeup is therefore individual and unique. Research shows that our genetic make up is responsible for many aspects of our abilities. These abilities help shape our lives and it is our lives and the experiences within those lives, the people we meet, the places we go to, etc. that give us our view of life. For instance, if you have a disability your experience of life will be very different from someone who does not have a disability. If you are unable to have children your view of life will probably be very different from someone who has lots of children. If you have cancer your experience of the world will be different from someone who does not and so on. But we are not just a collection of cells and DNA.

We also have brains—these are like our computers. They assimilate and sift through vast quantities of information and stimuli and provide us with answers and evaluations that have their basis in logic. But these are just aspects of our physical selves, and we are not just a physical entity.

We also have minds. This is the part of us that is responsible for our emotions and the emotional responses that we use to help us think, reason, evaluate and make decisions and judgements. Without our minds we would be little more basic than robots. This is another part of us that is unique and individual. Although we may think in a similar way to someone else we do not have exactly the same thought, phrased in exactly the same way. Even if we did we would interpret it slightly differently and we would react to it slightly differently because we would have an individual and unique emotional response to it. It is here, when we are looking at our emotional responses, that we realise this part of us cannot be described as physical. We can't see our minds, we can't measure them (yet) but it is our minds that begin to define us as a person and that begin to give us our "personality."

We have said that our minds are formed and shaped by our life experiences. But is it only our life experiences that shape our personality? We already appear to have our own "personality" from birth. If our minds were only formed by the experiences here how can we explain this?

We often bring up all our children in a reasonably identical way and yet they often turn out completely different. We can explain some of this by referring to our genetic background but there are other aspects of our lives that don't seem to conform to either genetics or the way we have been brought up. Some of us are born into poverty or extremely dysfunctional families yet we grow up to become really successful. Others who are born into these situations are never able to escape them. Children who are born into extreme wealth also develop in different ways despite similar upbringing and advantages.

It is also difficult to explain how some people seem to live a charmed existence whilst others seem to lurch from crisis to crisis however hard they try. Others seem to have relatively happy lives and others suffer appalling tragedies.

We can also look round and see that some people spend their lives trying to help others and yet others seem to spend their lives with little thought for others.

Finally there are those whose sole existence on the planet seems to be to cause misery and destruction.

These are just some of the ways in which the differences between people, even those from the same family, seem to be inexplicable.

So what is it that makes us totally unique and individual?

The part of us that is totally unique and totally individual is the part of us, that aspect of us, that we call our personality, that spark of some essence that is exclusively "us." We, the essence of us, is a form of energy that we call "spirit," and the part the philosopher Descartes called our soul. Because that is what our soul is—it is our spirit. So if our spirit is the essence of "us," where do we come from?

Where do we come from?

As spirits (or energy) we are neither male nor female and we exist in a place we call "Home." (This is the place religions refer to as "Heaven" or "Nirvana" or "Shangri-La," etc). "Home" is a highly-structured organised place and it exists on another vibration. It exists at the same time and in the same space as earth and we can go there at any time once we know how. We do this by meditation. When we meditate we are raising our level of consciousness. It is by raising our level of consciousness that we raise our vibratory level and by doing this we can project ourselves to Home.

It is there that we, as spirits, began our existence and it is there where we, as spirits, chose this life. Yes, we did say that we chose our lives. As spirits we would have been shown a "life" and asked if we would like to take that life and experience all the joys, trials, happiness and pain that make up that life.

The spiritual philosophy behind this idea of choice is not new. Plato, in "The Republic," recounts the story of Er who having "died" on the battlefield goes on a spiritual journey to the other world and then comes back to explain it to his fellow citizens. He describes how souls would choose their next life here and how the choice is made. Plato was greatly influenced by Pythagorean theories. Pythagoras was said to have gained his spiritual knowledge from the 22 years he spent in the temples of Egypt learning and being initiated into the ancient Egyptian Mysteries back in the 7th century BCE. These ancient pagan religions are understood to be the basis of Gnosticism which in turn can be seen as a forerunner of modern day spiritualism.

But why do we choose to take physical form in the first place? At Home there is no pain, no suffering, and no evil. There is nothing unpleasant at all. Because there are no negative emotions and experiences at Home it would be impossible for us (our spiritual selves) to know what negative means let alone how it feels. By negative emotions we are talking about hate, anger, despair, greed, jealousy, envy, intolerance, lust and the varying physical manifestations of those emotions—pain, suffering, depression, unhappiness, insecurity and control—and finally the effects of those negative emotions on the world as a whole—wars, famines, genocide, etc. So why do we have to experience these things and what will we gain from them?
In other words,

What is the purpose of life?

There are many reasons for us having to experience these things. The one thing you will find when you start asking questions about spirituality is that it is like an onion. No sooner have you found one meaning then you realise that this is just the start. As you begin to peel back the layers you find that under each one there is a deeper meaning and the further you go the more meanings you will find. At the same time they are still connected to the first meaning. As this is an introduction we are going to start by explaining the first layer.

First, for us to appreciate pure love and its accompanying positive emotions we must have something to compare it with. How can you know what "hot" is if you do not know what "cold" is? How can you know what happiness is if you have never been unhappy? More relevant perhaps is that you cannot appreciate being happy if you have never been unhappy. You

21

cannot appreciate warmth if you have never been cold. Without a physical form it would not be possible to experience any of these things. Therefore, to allow us to experience these things, we have to take physical form. We have chosen a particular body and a particular life to allow us to experience a particular set of emotions, sensations and feelings this time. In other words, the body we have and the life we have is the way we have chosen to experience these things. So the next time you look in the mirror and wonder why you don't look like Jordan or Brad Pitt, and you don't have David Beckham's talent or Bill Gates' money it is because YOU chose not to! The next time you wonder why your life is so eventful it is because YOU chose it to be like that. Scary isn't it? But maybe what you should be wondering is why on earth would I choose to look like this! Or why on earth would I choose to have these things happen? Why have I chosen this life, these experiences, these problems, these disabilities, these emotions?

Part of the answer of course is in what we have just said. We have chosen this body, this appearance, this life—with all its irritations, aggravations, problems, disasters, illnesses, etc just for that reason—to experience these things. But why on earth would we be so mad as to do that?

Why don't we all choose to live in perfect harmony, in happiness, in love and in light?

Again there are many reasons for this. The first, as we have said, is that, as spirits, we can experience that all the time at Home. The second reason is because we have not yet all reached the stage in our evolution where we can all see the benefit in that. We are all at different levels. Some spirits have been here many times and experienced many things. Others are just starting out so have yet to experience the vast array of emotions, feelings and sensations that the older spirits have already experienced. This is our university—the University of Life. And by learning we evolve, because that is really why we are here—to evolve. But we are also here to enjoy that learning process. Just think how much more we learn when we are enjoying ourselves. So it is also our playground and like all playgrounds, life is there in microcosm.

The playground bully who likes to control everyone, who likes to make himself look good at the expense of others, who uses his physical strength to hurt others. If we look around the world there are many examples of playground bullies. Then there are the teachers—some are good and some indifferent. Some want to share their knowledge and experience with anybody who will listen for the benefit of all. Others want to keep knowledge to themselves or corrupt it and use it for their own purposes, often to manipulate and control others. Then there are those who are insecure, those who are full of confidence, those who are popular and those who are unpopular. There are the people who seem to have everything, the people for whom everything always goes right and the people who seem to lurch from one crisis to another.

So why else would we want to choose to experience all these problems?

If we reach the age of 70 and have never had a problem in the whole of our lives how would we deal with it? We choose to experience all these problems because we use them to learn from. At some point our spirits would have experienced wars, and the emotions that go with that—hate, anger, violence, murder, mutilations, etc. If we look back at history we can see that the way our ancestors behaved is often abhorrent to us now. Even though there are people in the world who still carry out atrocities the majority of people now find such practices incomprehensible. We cannot possibly understand the mentality behind those actions because we have gone past that stage. We have progressed beyond those things. We have evolved to the level that we are at now. But we are still evolving. Our spirit is constantly evolving, striving to be the best it can be and to reach the heights of purity and perfection. We cannot do that at Home. We have to take physical form to experience all these things and we use these experiences to learn from. But we do not come here empty handed. We have tools that we have chosen to help

23

us while we are here. These tools are our gifts to ourselves. Part of our learning process here is to use the gifts we have chosen for the benefit of all and not to the detriment of others. We will explain more about these gifts in the next chapter.

Chapter 3

Is There Life After Death?

"The world exists only as an appearance. From beginning to end it is a playful game."

Shabistari, Sufi Sage

BEFORE we explain about our gifts we need to look at two other important and interconnected questions. These are: is there life after death, and if so where do we go?

And is there a God?

Let's start with:

Is there life after death and if so where do we go?

First we need to make sure we understand what the question means. What "life" are we referring to and what "death?" Presumably the "life" that we are referring to is the one we are experiencing at the moment—our physical life. We can't be talking about our spiritual life and death because our spirit is eternal. There is no life and death at Home—just calm peaceful evaluation of our physical lives and eternal existence. So let's assume we are referring to the lives that we are experiencing now. However, the lives that we are experiencing now are an illusion because our physical existence is an illusion. It is our spiritual existence that is real because we are essentially spirit that has taken physical form to experience physical things. Reality is at Home. Our lives here are our version of "Coronation Street" or "Emmerdale." Or if we are having a really bad time—"Eastenders!" We have chosen the character that we are going to play, we have read our script and how we fit into that story. We have met the spirits that are playing our parents, our spouse, our friends and our children if we have them. We have also met the people who hurt us, either physically or emotionally, and all the other spirits who will enter the story and play their part in helping us to evolve. We also meet all the people who we will help to evolve. This is what "life" is here.

If that is what life is, what is death?

"Is it [death] not the separation of soul and body? And to be dead is the completion of this; when the soul exists in herself, and is released from the body and the body is released from the soul, what is this but death."   (Phaedo [Jowett, 1937 vol. 1]: 447)

Presumably by death we mean the death of our bodies—you know, the body you are always complaining about. The one that is too fat, too thin, too tall, too short, is always ill, can't run quickly enough, isn't muscled enough, etc.! The body that we care so much about that we abuse it by filling it up with chemicals, alcohol, drugs, tobacco, processed food, insecticides, pesticides too much food, too little food, do we need to go on? This is the body that we are suddenly so attached to, that we love so much that we can't bear to let it go.

When we "die" it is our body that dies. It dies because we have reached the end of our part in the story. But our spirit doesn't die because it can't. All that happens is that the silver chord that attaches our spirit to this body is cut and we go Home. We have been written out of this bit because the "scriptwriter" has taken our character as far as he/she can go. It is also time for us to go Home and prepare for our next starring role and like all actors we need a good rest in between. After all, we have given our all and put everything we can into this performance. We have really believed in the part we have chosen. So now it's time for a rest to cleanse ourselves of all the negativity that we have picked up here and to reflect on how well we played our part, what we learned and perhaps how we could have done better. Then when we are fully rested we get to come back, (aren't we lucky!) and do it all again but this time with a different part, different scripts, different storylines, different gifts, etc.

Okay, this is a bit of a simplification but if we think of our lives in this respect it helps us to change our perceptions. By changing our perceptions we can change how we think. Our thoughts, words and actions are closely connected. If we change how we think our view of the world will change because our understanding of the world will change. Furthermore, cell science (the science of genes and cells) now recognises that our perception of our environment can directly control the activity of our genes. This is through a process known as epigenetic control. This radical new biology accepts that the body is not just a physical entity. Instead it views the mind and spirit as an integral part of the physical body. This is one of the reasons some people can have miraculous recoveries from what were perceived as life-threatening illnesses or permanent disabilities. By sending out different messages to our cells we can essentially help to reprogram them.

Seeing things differently can also help us to react to situations in a different way. If you know that the person who is jealous of you or whose behaviour is challenging is like this with your (spiritual) consent, and that you have already agreed that they will do this, you can react differently. The way we react to people is often conditioned by how they react to us. If they are angry and shouting at us it is very difficult to remain calm and reasoned. But if we can remain calm the outcome may be different. (We are not saying it definitely will be different but it might be!).

So if everything we have just said is true does this mean our lives are totally predetermined?

"The scope of the will is wider than that of the intellect; but instead of restricting it within the same limits, I extend its use to matters which I do not understand. Since the will is indifferent in such cases, it easily turns aside from what is true and good, and this is the source of my error and sin." Descartes (1596–1650)

This is actually a very important question because if everything we do is predetermined then it would mean that we are not responsible for anything we do. Sorry, but unfortunately it doesn't work like that. We have free choice. We have been given gifts and how we use these gifts is up to us. We can choose whether we use the gifts we have for good or for bad. Let's take the gift of impatience—we can either use our impatience in a negative way, for instance: standing in front of the microwave and complaining that it takes too long or being snappy and bad tempered with people who are not as quick or proficient as we would like—or we can use our impatience in a positive way. We can use it to help change things for the good. If our gift of impatience is channelled in a way that is for the good then we are using our free will to turn a seemingly negative emotion (a gift) we have been given in a positive way.

Let's take a more serious example

Hate is an extremely negative emotion and can be harmful to the person it is aimed at. But, more importantly, it is even more harmful to the person who is feeling it. If we spend our lives hating someone who we perceive has caused us some injustice, whose life are we wasting? While we are wasting all that energy, the person we hate is probably getting on with their lives totally unaware of how we feel. So who is being hurt by our hate? However, we can turn that hate into something positive. Rather than hating individuals, who generally have our spiritual agreement for their actions anyway, hate injustice, hate prejudice, hate poverty, hate violence, and hate war. Use "hate" in a positive way then it becomes a positive force for good. We can do this with all the gifts we have been given. Just think about it and we will find we can turn any of the apparently negative emotions we mentioned earlier into positive emotions and this is the reason they are called gifts. So although the gifts we have are predetermined the way we use them is up to us. That is our free choice.

Unconditional Love

Just as it is possible to use our negative gifts for good it is possible to use our positive gifts in a negative way. Let's take love. Love is the most powerful gift we have. But how many times do we see love used in a negative way. This happens in many ways but let's just look at a couple of aspects of this.

Love is supposed to be unconditional. This means that you love someone because of who they are. However, this does not work if the person whom you are giving unconditional love to does not understand and reciprocate. Part of love is tolerance. Tolerance is a positive gift and can be used in so many positive ways but if you are too tolerant it becomes a weakness because it becomes indifference. Tolerance is only really positive if everyone uses it in a positive way, otherwise it allows people to control you.

For example: when you fall in love you see the other person through rose tinted glasses! As the relationship develops you begin to see them in a more realistic light. Like you they are not perfect. They have their faults and strange ways. But the love you feel for them outweighs any negative feelings. This is unconditional love. However, unconditional love does not mean letting the other person hurt you nor does it mean making excuses for them when they do hurt you. Just as we have a duty to give unconditional love we have a right to expect unconditional love in return. Unconditional love applies not only to others but to our selves as well.

It also applies to people who are at the end of their physical lives. Often they remain, sometimes in pain or with little quality of life, because we are not ready or able to say goodbye. Unconditional love means letting go. Until they go back to spirit they cannot evolve. Their spirit will remain attached to their body even though they have finished all they came here to do. They are staying because it is an experience we have chosen to have and because they love us unconditionally, yet if we love them unconditionally we would choose to let them go.

The majority of parents would say that they love their children unconditionally. But loving your children unconditionally does not mean letting them do exactly as they wish. Like us they are here to learn and evolve. Our responsibility to them is to ensure that we bring them up to be independent and to pass on our values and our morality. But all good relationships have to be balanced. We have to learn to give and to receive and we have to teach our children this message too. If we give all the time and never receive not only will we make the other person extremely selfish but we will also deny them the gift of giving.

If we teach our children that we will give them anything yet they don't have to do anything in return we are bringing them up with a false picture of life. Life is all about finding the balance between giving and receiving. This does not mean that we are putting conditions on our love. Part of loving someone is respecting them. If we don't respect ourselves how can we respect each other and how can we teach our children to respect themselves and each other? The message we should be giving them is that everyone deserves love and respect including ourselves. Without self- respect and self-love we become insecure. Insecurities lead to us trying to control others. Because we do not feel good about ourselves we cannot imagine that other people like us. We all know people who abuse friendships because of their feelings of insecurity. They become friends with you and then start to isolate you from your other friends by making themselves seemingly indispensable and repeating supposed conversations they have had with your friends. You begin to believe them and when your previous friends complain you think they are to blame. Although this may sound like behaviour that only happens in the playground unfortunately it is more common in adult life than it should be. It is often carried into our marriages and partnerships and is the basis for the majority of abusive domestic relationships.

We, all of us, need to ensure our children grow up with a positive self- image. If we fail in this message our children may well be drawn into abusive relationships, either as the victim or the abuser. If the message that we are giving does not explain the balance between giving and receiving and is based on using love as a means of control our children will continue the cycle of abusive relationships that make up so much of society.

These are just a few examples of how we can use our thoughts and emotions (our gifts) in a more positive way. But to do this we need balance.

Balance

We have looked at how important it is for everyone to find the balance between too much tolerance and too little otherwise it has a negative impact on our private lives. The same can be said of our public lives. We are often told that tolerance is a virtue. But is that always the case? Could it be argued that tolerance is actually a weakness, a luxury that we cannot afford, because if it is carried to its ultimate is often a sign of indifference?

Our society is based on tolerance and the celebration of diversity. But this only works if all members of society share those values and adhere to that code and if there is balance. If there are members of the society who are tolerant to the point of indifference, or too intolerant, or who view that tolerance as a weakness, society itself is weakened and this opens the doors to extremism.

Western liberal democracy is based on the belief that we are all free, rational individuals who have the right to live our lives with minimal interference from the State. This belief encourages us to be tolerant of other's beliefs, lifestyles, etc. However, like unconditional love, tolerance only works if it is universal. If it is not universal it allows those whose intentions are not liberal and democratic to undermine the very foundations of our society. We only have to look at the history of the 20th century to see how the tolerance embedded in liberalism has led to the growth of totalitarian regimes. The growth of religious fundamentalism is no different. Religious fundamentalism is just another form of totalitarian ideology that, in essence, is no different from Nazism or Communism. They all set out to repress the basic freedoms and liberties of democracy and to control the way their citizens think. They all exhort their followers to fight for their "nation/ belief system/way of life" because they are under threat from outside influences. They all wish to return to a past era in which life was apparently better and they all see the root of their current problems as a direct result of the tolerant attitudes embedded in liberal democracy. Furthermore they all portray themselves as victims of liberal democracy rather then aggressors.

One way of looking at religious fundamentalists would be to compare them to perpetrators of domestic violence. Most people would accept that those who abuse people in relationships are bullies. They become bullies because they are insecure and one of the main characteristics of bullies is their lack of personal responsibility—the "poor me" syndrome—"I hit you because you made me." People who are secure have no need to control others and the same applies to organisations, corporations, nations and belief systems. Religious fundamentalists wish to impose their beliefs on others. They do not believe in tolerance nor do they believe in the right to believe in anything other than the view they are preaching. Presumably, if they were secure in the truth or veracity of their belief they would not seek to impose it on others because rational argument would suffice. But it is this belief in rationality as well as the capacity for tolerance that is at the heart of the problem. Most rational people cannot understand why someone would choose to impose a repressive regime on others so do not recognise the dangers. We see things from our own perspective and if we enjoy the benefits of a liberal democracy we find it difficult to understand those who wish to be told how to think. The same thing happened in the 1930s when very few people could see the dangers in the growth of the Third Reich.

The problem for liberal democracies, belief systems, organisations and individuals is how to maintain tolerance of alternative ideologies, beliefs and individualism without allowing this tolerance to be seen as a fundamental weakness and therefore something to be replaced with a dictatorship. Unfortunately, doing nothing is not an option. Doing nothing, pandering to the insecurities of those who do not believe in the basic freedoms we take for granted, is not tolerance; it is indifference. Indifference sends out signals that we do not believe in our freedoms. So many in two generations died for us to have these freedoms— are they not worth defending?

There is considerable controversy over how the Human Rights Act is being interpreted. It appears that the rights of the few are being given precedent over the rights of the majority. Human Rights seem to have taken precedence over anything else and it seems the courts now have more powers than the elected governments of our countries. Not only has this led to calls that the rights of the accused and the rights of victims need to be more balanced, it also has implications for our security as a nation. If we believe in freedom then we must also believe that we have the right to protect ourselves against those who do not believe in our values, freedoms and way of life and who seek to change it through undemocratic means.

Most people would also agree that there is imbalance in the way our financial institutions work and in the way we redistribute our wealth and resources. This leads to taxation and benefit policies that are frequently viewed as unfair. Often this perception is as much to do with how the policies are presented, but equally many are not thought out properly and are unfair. To address inequalities, those who are perceived as unequal are often given special rights. This can be seen in instances where positive vetting is used to increase the number of women in parliament or when cultural or religious minorities ask for special treatment under the law. The same applies to institutions.

In response to concerns about high taxation and abuses of the benefit system a government will be elected that reduces taxation to a minimum with the resulting cut in benefits and public services. Eventually this policy will be seen as unfair and the next government will be elected on promises to raise taxation, either directly or indirectly and increases benefits and public services. However, as both policies are seen as unfair to a proportion of the population, and a true balance is never reached the next government will reduce taxation and reduce public services and so on. The problems are then exacerbated by the scaremongering of certain interest groups and by the scapegoating of sections of society by those who wish to absolve themselves of responsibility.

At present the ills of society are being blamed on our young people. However, our children learn by example. If we do not like the way they behave perhaps we should look more closely at our own behaviour and the examples we are setting.

Other sections of society who are regularly targeted are single mothers and immigrants. Many single mothers are single through no fault of their own and are doing their best to bring up their children without the children's father. If we trace our family history back far enough most of us are immigrants and the majority of us are descended from economic migrants. The only difference between us and the newer wave of immigrants is that they are more visible because their skin is a different colour. We need to move away from this collective scapegoating and accept that there will always be people who will abuse the system. They exist in all walks of society, in both sexes, in all classes, and in all economic and cultural groups. Some have just lost their way or are misguided, others abuse these things deliberately.

So if all these apparently negative emotions are just the way we are using our gifts is there really something that can be called evil?

The deliberate abuse and misuse of the positive gifts leads to restrictions and legislation where previously none was needed. This can be seen in the increasing restrictions on activities that used to be part of normal life or in legislation that is brought in hastily in response to a "public outcry." It is deliberate because by causing mistrust and intolerance, negative energy is able to increase and multiply.

So the answer to this question is yes. There is something in the world that can be called evil. It is a scientific fact that everything has an opposite. If you believe that there is good in the world you have to accept that there must also be evil. How else would you know what good was? What would you use to measure "good" against? We are back to "hot" and "cold," "light" and "dark" again. You cannot physically see "good" but you don't doubt its existence so why would you doubt the existence of "evil." For some reason we all find it easier to accept the concept of a power that is light and love (God, for want of a better word) than to accept the existence of a power that is dark and evil. This is because not believing in its existence allows it to grow. If anything, "evil" is probably easier to see than good. It can be seen in the way we treat each other, in the way we treat those who do not have access to equal power, in the way we treat children, women, and the elderly, in the way we treat those who do not have the same views, beliefs, lifestyles, etc and it can be seen most of all in the way we treat our world.

34

"All that is necessary for the triumph of evil is that good men do nothing." (Edmund Burke 1729 -1797)

Evil is not a figment of religion's imagination. By refusing to accept its existence evil will flourish and become stronger. There is a difference between someone who just makes a mistake and someone who deliberately sets out to cause suffering with no remorse. Just as we chose our lives there are spirits who chose to evolve in the other direction and who chose lives that are evil. Yes, we know it sounds like something out of a horror film but can you honestly look round the world and not see examples of what we are describing? Again we want to emphasis the difference between those who allow their negative emotions to rule them and those who are genuinely evil. Unfortunately those who are genuinely evil use negative emotions to spread their power. By using positive thoughts and positive emotions we can begin to reverse this damage.

We are here to evolve and we do this, in part, through the experiences we have on the earth plane. If we have a problem in our personal lives we try to learn from it so that we don't have to experience it again. But we are not just individuals with personal lives; we are also citizens of the world with a responsibility to others. Spiritualists, like all other religions, believe that we are all one, that we are all responsible for our own thoughts, words and actions and that we are here to help each other. This applies on both a personal and a global basis. One of the gifts we are given to use is tolerance. But like all our gifts they can be used for good or for bad. Although we have not eradicated domestic violence it is at least being addressed. Ignoring it did not work. If we, as individuals, do nothing to defend our freedoms, then we may find that we as a society lose these freedoms.

Spiritualism is growing—the direction in which it grows is up to us. We tell people that it is a way of life. If we genuinely believe that, then we have to take spiritualism into the community, become involved in politics and defend our values, beliefs and freedoms. We cannot detach spirituality from public life because that creates a vacuum and it is the spiritual vacuum in our present day society that is opening the door to religious fundamentalism of all persuasions. Nor can we detach ourselves from politics. We are responsible for our world and only we can change it. As the advert says—if you don't "do" politics—you don't "do" life!

And this leads nicely onto the next question which people frequently ask when they see so much misery and suffering. The next chapter asks "is there a God?"

Chapter 4

Is There a God?

"...the mere fact that I exist and have within me an idea of a most perfect being... provides a very clear proof that God indeed exists."
Descartes 1596–1650

WHEN we look at the state of our planet, at the injustice, the wars, the seemingly endless cruelty, sadness and pain and all the natural disasters we often ask ourselves this. But if you think about what we have just said and you change your perceptions accordingly it all starts to make some kind of sense. Our spirits have taken physical form to enable them to evolve. Because it is only through experiencing everything that we can evolve we have to take physical form otherwise we cannot experience anything and so cannot evolve. We will not evolve if all we have is happiness and light. First, we can experience this as spirits all the time at Home. Secondly, if we don't experience anything other than happiness and light how will we know this is what we are experiencing because we will have nothing to compare it with? Thirdly, because we are all at differing stages in our evolution many things that happen are beyond our comprehension. We have evolved past that stage. Finally, there are those people who are truly evil and whose sole purpose is to evolve further down the path away from the light—the path towards darkness. Remember that it as an accepted scientific fact that everything has an opposite, so if there is a path to the light it is logical that there is also a path to the darkness. You cannot accept that there is one without also accepting that there is the opposite.

So if that explains the suffering we cause each other what about natural disasters?

We are all part of one great consciousness, one Great Mind. This includes the planet. The planet is also evolving and changing. Everything we do impacts on the planet. On one hand there are the results of our physical activities. Cutting down the rainforest is destroying the planet's lungs. Deforestation in other parts of the world leads to mudslides when there is heavy rain. Our exploitation of the planet causes floods and droughts and these in turn lead to other catastrophes. (We are not going to turn this into a lecture on the environment because we are not scientists and the statistics are there for anyone who wants to read them). But on the whole, our efforts to control the planet have been an unmitigated disaster.

On the other hand there are the results of our emotional activities. These thoughts and emotions manifest themselves in the physical ways I have just mentioned, but they also affect the planet in other ways.

Thoughts

"We are what we think. All that we are arises with our thoughts. With our thoughts we create the world." The Buddha

Your thoughts are a very powerful form of energy. How many times have you suddenly thought about someone you haven't heard from in years and then they contact you? Or you ring someone and they tell you they were just about to ring you? How many times do you pick up on what others are thinking? Do you say what someone else is thinking? Do they say what you are thinking? What about the saying "be careful what you wish for!" How many times have you wished for something and it happens but not in the way you wished for it. Every time we have a thought we are sending out a message to the universe saying this is what we would like to happen.

That is why it is so important to think positive thoughts. There is a saying that "like attracts like." Nowhere is this more true than in our thoughts. Positive thoughts attract positive energy. Unfortunately the reverse is also true. Negative thoughts attract negative energy. Every time you worry or visualise something terrible happening you are sending out a message saying that this is what you would like to happen. Conversely, every time you send out a positive thought you are saying that is what you would like to happen.

However, it can be very difficult to control our thoughts. But our thoughts often lead to words and our words lead to actions. We have already looked at the destructive effects of hate. Hate is often caused by jealousy. But as with hate, jealousy is more harmful to the person who is feeling it. Jealousy can lead to people acting in ways that they would not normally consider. People feel jealous for many reasons but it is usually because they feel inadequate or feel they are missing out in some way. But we have all chosen our lives. We all have different pathways and different goals to achieve. Their pathway is not the same as ours. Although we are all here to evolve we will not all be travelling at the same speed or even in the same direction on the same road. When we travel to Scotland we do not all take the M1. Some of us use the motorway for a little while and then we might stop for a break or take a side road. Others may start off on the A1 or a side road and then come on to the motorway. Others may not use the motorway at all but they still get there. We all still get there whatever route we use and however many deviations we take. We do not worry about the route others are taking, we do not feel it is a competition or worry about whether their car is bigger or faster than our own. We just concentrate our own journey. The same applies to life. We should be concentrating on our own journey and not worrying about others.

But jealousy, like hate, is just another gift. By changing our perceptions of why we are here we will realise that the only people who are a threat to our lives, happiness, fulfilment and evolution are ourselves. Sending out negative thoughts attracts negative energy to the sender. By allowing our thoughts, words and actions to be ruled by jealousy we are blocking positive energy and the positive opportunities that result from this. The person we are jealous of may initially be hurt by our actions, but because their thoughts are positive they will move on and take the opportunities that open up for them.

It is also important that we look at the way we phrase our thoughts when we are asking for help. If you ask for help you will always get it but you do need to be careful what you are asking for. How many times do we say "give me strength" when things are difficult? The problem with this is that you only become stronger by dealing with situations that make you strong. So asking for strength is like asking for all sorts of difficult situations and experiences that will literally "give you strength." How many times do we wish we could tell when people are lying to us? Again, the problem with this is we just end up meeting lots of people who lie to us so that we learn to discern between the truth and lies.

Furthermore, when asking for help we have to make some effort ourselves. If we just asked for things and were given them without having to do anything we would end up lazy and spoilt and we would not learn anything. If, for example, you ask to find another job, it won't happen unless you make some effort to find another job. It won't just fall into your lap.

Often we ask for help and someone will come into our lives who will provide that help. But when it is time for that person to go, for whatever reason, we find it difficult to let go. They have been sent to us for a reason. They may have been in our lives for a short while or many years. We no longer need them and they no longer need us. It is time to move on and meet new people and have new experiences. This will not happen if you cannot let go. This means letting go emotionally as well as physically.

It is also pointless saying you "want" something as it just gives you the experience of "wanting." You have to say "I choose." But be careful how you use the word "choose." All choices have consequences and if you are not specific you may get what you asked for but not in the way you meant! For example: If you say "I choose to lose weight" you have to make it clear that you mean through willpower, exercise and healthy eating otherwise you may find that you suddenly have a lot of emotional or physical problems that result in you losing weight!

Another example of not thinking choices through is mankind's desire to control the planet and its weather. We are now at the point where our lifestyles, industries and technologies do exactly that, but presumably the mess the planet is in is not what we intended. So, we should always choose with care.

However, it is not all bad news. Saying "I choose to improve the world in which I am living" could change your life in so many ways that you will look back on that moment as the defining moment when your life and the planet changed for the better. But how closely are our thoughts connected to our emotions?

Emotions

Which makes you feel better? Watching a film or television programme that makes you laugh or watching a film or television programme which is full of violence and swearing?

What about the music we listen to? Do you feel better listening to relaxing uplifting music or music that is loud, repetitive and strident? How about music that has destructive or very negative lyrics or music that is sad? The Welcome Trust has carried out research that shows gentle, happy music helps people in hospital recover more quickly and are recommending that hospitals play this type of music on the wards. Many spiritualist centres play lively uplifting music because it raises the vibrations and allows spirits that work on the light to come through more easily. If music can affect people to this extent what effect does some of the music we listen to have on us?

In a world that is so negative shouldn't we be doing all that we can to raise the vibrations to a more positive level? Music, films, television programs, the news, the internet and the media in general all impact on our lives in a much greater way than in previous generations. At present there is a proliferation of television mediums and psychic programmes. Whilst this has helped to raise the profile of spiritualism in many positive ways it has also added to the prevailing perception that spiritualism is just entertainment. It must be very difficult for TV mediums to ensure that the messages and information they know they are there to impart are not subsumed under the producers' need to keep viewing figures at a certain level. We, as viewers, have a responsibility to ensure they are able to do this. The danger of allowing commercial interests to trivialise mediumship is that the real message is lost. This can happen despite the best efforts of the medium.

Furthermore, advances in science and communication technology mean we can find out what is happening in any part of the world in an instant. Theoretically this should mean we are all better informed. But are we? If we do not have access to all the information we are not able to make informed decisions and choices. Time and commercial constraints mean that news producers have little choice in deciding which issues we should hear about. This sometimes leads to news broadcasts that seem to prioritise trivial things and other, more important issues are either not covered or relegated to less important positions. For instance: after the world cup in 2006 the resignation of David Beckham as England captain was considered more important than the death of two British soldiers in Afghanistan. Many national news broadcasts are criticised for their parochial content or for putting items of international importance after national issues. This has led to some critics claiming that television is little more than "opium for the masses" and there are many more who consider society to be "dumbing down."

We cannot blame the media if we do not like the direction or content of their products. We are all responsible for the contents of our programmes, video games, the news, films and music because we are all consumers. Without us, the consumer, there would not be a media. In the case of news broadcasts we have the option of complaining or watching an alternative news broadcast that does give us the information that we want. In the case of violent or negative television programmes and films it is claimed that science is just interpreting our thoughts and emotions and allowing us the luxury of watching from the outside. But is it? Is the media reflecting the world or does the world reflect what it sees in the media?

We are all at different levels of evolution. While some people have no trouble distinguishing between fact and fiction, others, especially our children and those who are vulnerable, find it more difficult. Whether violence on television, films or video games encourages more violence is disputed but logically it must desensitise us to a certain extent. Organisations that come face to face with violence and death every day have access to regular counselling to deal with its negative effects. Viewers do not.

There are also concerns that because we have become desensitised not only can we become addicted to the violence that we see, but we can also think that it is normal acceptable behaviour or even that it is funny. Violence is usually the response of someone who is unable to express themselves in any other way. It can be out of frustration or because it is simply the only way they know. It may be that violence has always helped them achieve their goal or even that they enjoy it. As we evolve we can see that violence is never the answer. We can also see that it is not funny. Laughter is a positive gift and should be used as such. Our sense of humour is so that we can laugh at ourselves, not at someone else's pain.

A recent UNICEF report stated that children in Britain are the poorest in Europe, not just financially but emotionally and spiritually. Whilst we are protective of our children's physical safety almost to the point of paranoia, their mental, emotional and spiritual well being is ignored. This concern for their physical safety has led to a generation of children who spend much of their time cocooned indoors apparently "safely" watching television and playing computer games. But whilst they sit indoors we are exposing them to and in some cases bombarding them with images of violence and cruelty. Our most popular television programmes, video games and internet sites are based on humiliation and a kind of voyeurism that delights in watching people make fools of themselves or hurt each other. Children learn by example and these are the kind of examples they are copying. It is little wonder that some of our children have lost their sense of direction. Our children are our responsibility and it is up to us to show them a different way.

Violence in our thoughts, words and actions stems from hate, which in turn stems from jealousy and insecurity. Jealousy and insecurity stem from low self-esteem and low self-esteem is something that comes from a lack of self-love and self-respect.

Both women and men suffer from low self-esteem and it can be expressed in many different ways. Whereas men tend to articulate their self-destructive behaviour in ways that hit outwards towards others, women tend to do the opposite. Their violence is often internalised and aimed at themselves and can take a variety of forms. Not only do they physically self-harm by cutting themselves they also starve themselves or overeat. They can also allow themselves to stay in abusive relationships because they do not believe that they really deserve better.

Men who suffer from low self-esteem can be abusers or serially unfaithful. They tend to sabotage their relationships because they do not really think they are worthy of love. But it is not only their relationships they destroy. They constantly set challenges in work and in life that are unrealistic because failing reinforces their lack of self-worth. And it is not just the damage to other people. Those who lack self-esteem and self-worth are extremely vulnerable. They fall prey to all kinds of abuse including those who indoctrinate them into committing atrocities for the sake of some mythical cause or some mythical reward in the hereafter.

Until we can break this cycle in ourselves we cannot change our society because our children will grow up making the same mistakes we have made. By setting a different example to our children they will see that violence to others and to themselves is not the answer to anything, and our world will begin to change. This applies not just to the way we treat each other but also to the way we treat our planet. By changing our perceptions we will bring our children up with a different understanding and consequently they will grow up with different values. This will speed up the process of our evolution, and when we have all evolved to a higher level we will begin to reverse the damage we are doing to our world and to each other. Until we do this nothing will change and unfortunately doing nothing is no longer an option. As we will see in the next chapter, we are running out of time.

Chapter 5

Evolution

"Whatever a man sows, that he will also reap."　　　　　St Paul

WE cannot survive in physical form without the planet. Our physical bodies need physical things to survive—oxygen, nitrogen, water, food, light, warmth, etc. Our planet is getting old. Unfortunately we don't have a very good record when it comes to dealing with the "old." When something is old we throw it out and replace it with something new. At present this is not an option with our planet. However, we are already looking for other planets to move to and developing the technology to adapt them for human existence. But if we have not evolved any further than we are now what makes us think it is going to be any better elsewhere? If we cannot take care of the world we do have, should we have the right to expect another planet to ruin? We celebrate "youth" and "youth culture" and instead of treating our elderly people with respect we treat them as a nuisance. But in spiritual terms is that a good idea? It was "us" as young spirits that carried out all the horrendous things throughout the planet's history that we now look on with abhorrence. We have now evolved past that stage. As older spirits we know that we have to take care of our planet. But the planet will only be taken care of when world consciousness evolves. For that to happen we have to evolve and one of the ways we do that is when we die. This is when we go Home, evaluate what we have learnt and move forward to the next stage.

We are now at the crossroads. If we do not begin to reverse the damage we have caused the planet in the next ten to fifteen years it will be too late. To save the planet we need to be evolving faster than we are. To enable this to take place large scale "natural" disasters happen. Those who are still here begin to rethink their attitudes to the planet and for a little while we all become more aware of what we are doing to both the planet and each other. We also become much more spiritual as we search for some kind of meaning and explanation. This again raises the consciousness of the world and despite the suffering, or maybe because of it, we all become more spiritually aware.

But we have very short memories and the world at the moment is a very unstable place. Everything is in a state of change. This in itself is not a bad thing provided those changes are for the benefit of all. Unfortunately this is not what is happening. The world is becoming even more polarised into those who have and those who have not, the rich and the poor, the weak and the strong. Although our resources are not infinite there is more than enough to go round if we could only learn to share, to become more tolerant, to use the gifts we have been given wisely and for the benefit of all. Although pain and suffering helps us all to evolve it does not have to be that way. We can also evolve without this suffering if we can only change our perceptions of why we are here. If we all accept that we are collectively responsible for every life, for every thought, word and action, for everything that happens on this planet, we can begin to make changes.

Of course this means compromise, this means sitting down and discussing things that we don't agree on. Because we all have different life experiences and thus different perceptions there are bound to be disagreements. But many conflicts can be overcome if people start to listen to each other, and to be honest with each other. Many conflicts are caused because we can only see things from our own point of view or because we only think of our own self-interest. If we change our perceptions and realise that we are all one spirit, we are all part of the Great Mind, this one great consciousness, self-interest takes on a whole new meaning.

It is in all our interests to look after each other, to ensure that we all have enough to eat, clean water to drink, warmth, heat and light. It is in all our interests to end poverty, to end war, to end pain and suffering.

Even if you find it hard to grasp the idea that we are all one—think about the concept of reincarnation. Most of the world's religions and belief systems accept that reincarnation is or can be possible. If this is the case we are going to have to come back again. So isn't it better that we sort out the problems now? Otherwise we could be "the minority;" we could be "the starving;" we could be the suffering millions.

From a political point of view the world is now a very small place. Poverty leads to competition for scarce resources and ultimately to violence. Globalisation now means that those in impoverished countries or those living under violent regimes can see images of a better life in other countries. People flee poverty and violent countries and seek asylum in other more stable countries. This puts pressure on the host communities and this leads to intolerance. Intolerance ultimately leads to more violence and destabilisation and so on.

Helping people to stabilise and regenerate their own countries makes much more sense. Many migrants would prefer to stay in their own countries rather then suffer the hardships of emigrating and having to start a new life in countries that are often hostile. But many see no option. Like all of us they are simply trying to make a better life for themselves and their children. Ending economic exploitation of the poorest countries also makes more sense and there are already moves in that direction. But for it to work we all need to change our views about what is essential for our existence and what we can comfortably do without.

Finally, from a scientific point of view, global warming is caused by all of us on the planet. As the Greenpeace website explains:

A certain amount of additional warming—about 1.3° Celsius (2.3° Fahrenheit) compared to pre-industrial levels—is probably inevitable because of emissions so far. Limiting warming to under 2° C (3.6°F) is considered vital to preventing the worst effects of climate change.

If our greenhouse gas emissions are not brought under control, the speed of climate change over the next hundred years will be faster than anything known since before the dawn of civilization.

There is a very real possibility that climate feedback mechanisms will result in a sudden and irreversible climate shift. No one knows how much global warming it would take to trigger such a "doomsday scenario."

There is little point in some countries cutting their carbon emissions if other countries make no effort to decrease theirs and in some cases actively increase it. If we don't all work together nothing will change and we will all suffer.

Yes, it sounds very selfish to think like this but isn't it just another way of turning our "gift" of selfishness into something positive?

The world we live in is our responsibility. We have chosen for it to be like it is. If we don't like it then we have the power to change it. To change things we have to start taking responsibility for ourselves, to take responsibility for the way we think, to take responsibility for the way we act. Changing our perceptions of what we are, why we are here, and our views of life and death and "God" are the first steps. It is no longer acceptable to blame God for our suffering, we chose our world—if we don't like it then it is up to us to change it!

Personal responsibility

We have just said that the world is like it is because we have chosen it to be this way and that if we don't like it we should change it. You may think that this doesn't really concern you and that you are not really interested in politics. But politics affect every aspect of your life from the food you eat to the air that you breathe. If you don't change things who will? You may think there is nothing you can do but we live in a democracy and you are a citizen of that democracy. If you accept the rights and benefits that democracy gives you must also accept that you have duties as a citizen. If you are stranded in a war-torn country you expect your government to help you. If you are caught up in a disaster who do you expect to rescue you? If you are a victim of crime who do you go to for help? We are the people—all of us.

We have to take responsibility for the way our world is and

48

we can start by looking at the way our own country is run. Let's look at democracy. Democracy is supposed to be government for the people by the people. The lawmakers are separate from the administrators of the law and everyone is supposed to have equal access to justice. The concept of democracy is that we all work together to make the world the kind of place we all want to live in.

In its original form it was all about individuals working together, discussing issues and finding a solution that everybody felt happy with. It had nothing to do with political parties. Many parish councils still work this way. However, when we look at the world's most powerful democracies are they really a good advert for democracy?

How many of us voted at the last election? Our governments are elected by a minority of the people which means the majority of us are not represented. Political parties distort democracy because individuals within political parties are not allowed to speak as individuals—they have to toe the party line. We often end up voting for people whose views we don't really agree with just because they are better than "the other party." Think about your own political views. Do you agree with every single thing that "your" party says? Most people have a belief system that covers a broad spectrum of opinions and doesn't conform to just one party. Maybe that is one of the reasons people no longer bother to vote. After all if someone came to paint all the rooms in your house and said he was going to paint your kitchen and bathroom black would you go along with it because you liked the rest? Would you pay him for it? (Apologies to those who might like to have a black bathroom and kitchen—it's just a daft analogy—almost as daft as giving control of our lives to someone who only says some things we agree with!)

Proportional representation has been a contentious issue for many years and the two main political parties have always opposed it on the grounds that it wouldn't work (other countries do it), it would be too complicated (are we not as clever as the populations of other countries then?) or it is too expensive to introduce. It can be introduced gradually and it doesn't need to be any more expensive than the present system. Start by changing politics at local level. Introduce proportional representation and independent candidates at one local election. See what happens. Yes, there is always the danger of an extremist element being elected but that can happen now. There is much less chance of that happening if we all have our say—if we all feel that we are being listened to—if we all feel that our views are represented.

Far from empowering people, democracy in its present form takes power away from people. Do we really need political parties to run our district, borough and county councils? Maybe local politics should be just that—local. People should stand independently on local issues. By working together they would be working for the good of the whole community not just a few. Of course this means listening to the people they represent, listening to each other and reaching majority decisions in the interests of the majority. Working together would remove the need to continually blame each other for any perceived mistakes because they would all be collectively responsible for the decisions that are made.

Seeing politicians accepting responsibility for their decisions would then set an example to us all. Instead of blaming someone when we have an accident we could accept that it might have been our fault or just an accident. Whilst we are not saying that there are some cases where people should be made to pay compensate, does compensation have to be in everything? The present culture of suing is changing our lives beyond recognition. Because everybody is so worried that they will be sued if they make a mistake or do not cover ever angle we are prevented from doing things that we have done for years. How many times have we heard people say that all they really wanted was an apology? But apologising would mean admitting responsibility so the organisation is advised not apologise. The case goes to court and millions of pounds are wasted. Whilst insurance was originally brought in to protect us it has now become a millstone round our necks. We have lost our personal sense of responsibility and unfortunately we are bringing up our children to see this as the right way to behave.

By changing our perceptions of what we are, where we come from and why we are here, we can make considerable changes to both our planet and the societies in which we live. It is our world and we sincerely believe that it is now time to make changes but we don't expect you to take our word for it. In the next chapter we show you how to meditate. Once you are able to meditate you will be able to ask the questions yourself.

Chapter 6

Meditation

"Be empty. Be still.
Watch everything just come and go.
Emerging from the source—returning to the source.
This is the way of nature.
This is the fulfilment of your destiny.
Know that which never changes.
This is enlightenment."

Lao Tzu, Taoist Sage

IN the first five chapters we have looked at the philosophy that underpins our spiritual framework. This spiritual philosophy incorporated both science and politics and showed us how they can all work together. Its now time to look at some practical ways that we can address some of the issues raised in those chapters. We have said that you should find answers for yourselves. We are now going to teach you how to do that. We will start with meditation.

Everywhere we look there are people, magazines and television programmes telling us that anyone can meditate and anyone can talk to spirit guides. This is perfectly true. But what they don't tell you is that before you do this you need to protect yourself.

What is meditation?

"Meditate and realise that this world is full of the presence of God."
Shvetashvatara Upanishad—Hindu Scripture

When we meditate we are raising our consciousness to another vibration. Yes, we know that sounds complicated—but it isn't—it's just a matter of practising like anything else. The spirits we wish to talk to are those that work on the vibration of love and light, but there are other spirits out there who do not work on this vibration. You have only to look around the world to see the effect of negative vibrations on the planet—the last thing we need to do is to add to these.

How do you protect yourself?

Protection is straightforward. All you need to do is imagine a tiny seed located within your chest. This seed can be seen to be a little white light. Visualise this white light getting brighter and bigger. Every time you breathe out this light grows brighter and bigger until eventually it becomes like a brilliant white egg that surrounds you. Imagine that anyone looking at you would not be able to see you—all they would see would be a brilliant white light. Then ask (in your head) that only the highest, the purest and the best come through and that's it—that is your protection. Simple isn't it!

Follow this with a request that healing goes out to the planet and all those on it and then add the names of those you know who might need healing, both physically and emotionally. By this we just mean ask in your own words—just like you would in a prayer. (i.e. Please send healing to the planet and to John, Mabel, etc). The reason you are doing this at the beginning of your meditation is that spirit work on three levels of vibration. The highest is the healing vibration, the next is the spiritual and philosophical vibration and the lowest is the psychic and clairvoyant vibration. By asking for healing at the beginning you are automatically raising your vibration to the highest level. Of course you have to mean it. There is no point asking for healing for the planet and friends if you don't actually mean it! When you have done this you are ready to begin your meditation.

Why is it dangerous to drink alcohol or take drugs before meditating?

We all know the dangers to our bodies of drinking excess alcohol and taking drugs (both illegal drugs and prescription drugs) but it isn't just our bodies that are affected. When we drink alcohol or take drugs we can change our perceptions of reality. (We would like to stress that we are not suggesting that you stop taking your prescription drugs—just be a little careful when meditating if they cause drowsiness or are specifically intended to alter perception). If our perception of reality has changed we render ourselves much more likely to pick up on the negative elements we have just mentioned. We only have to look around us to see the effects of excess alcohol and "recreational" drugs under everyday circumstances. This is heightened by any attempt to communicate consciously with Spirit. When under the influence of drugs and alcohol we are not in control of our faculties. This is the perfect opportunity for negative thoughts and emotions and negative energies to come through. If we try to communicate with Spirit under these conditions we are asking for trouble. (See Chapter 8—Ouija boards)

When can I meditate?

You can meditate whenever you have time, but you should obviously make sure that when you meditate you are safe. Do not meditate when you are driving, travelling on your own or anywhere else that needs you to be aware of your surroundings. If you are using candles make sure they are on a secure surface and they cannot fall over or catch anything alight. It is also a good idea to try and meditate at the same time of day if at all possible as your guides will then come through quicker, but it is not essential.

One other point to remember is that your guides will be really pleased and excited that you have chosen to start communicating with them. They may try to come through at times when it is not convenient. There is no time at Home but there is on the earth plane and you would prefer them not to wake you up in the middle of the night! This is not a problem. Just tell them it is not convenient and ask them to come back at a time of your choosing. Be firm but polite.

Can I meditate on my own?

If you have never meditated before it is often a good idea to go to a group as you will have someone to talk you through it and the energy will be higher if there are more people. But it is not essential. The most important thing is to find a time where you will not be disturbed. Take the phone off the hook and switch off your mobile phone. There are very few things that are so urgent that they can't wait half an hour. Put on some nice relaxing music and make yourself comfortable in a chair or if you find it more relaxing lie on the floor. The volume of the music is up to you. At the beginning some people find it easier if the music is loud as it drowns out outside noise. Of course, don't have it so loud that you annoy the neighbours or they will be hammering on your door or wall which rather defeats the object. Other people prefer to have it just as background noise. There is no set rule. It's your choice.

How do I know I am meditating?

The point of meditation is to relax you and allow your spirit some time away from the cares of the world. It is to revitalise and re-energise your spirit. People often have completely the wrong idea about what will happen when they meditate. The first time you will probably find it hard to relax but don't get frustrated and don't give up. If you really find you cannot shake off all the thoughts that are flying round your head then don't try. Just let your mind wander. Don't give any thought too much time but just let the thoughts drift in and out of your head. You will still find that you feel relaxed when you finish. You can try wrapping up all your problems in some paper, putting them in a basket and watching them float away (this is a visualisation of course), or putting them into individual bubbles and letting them float away. If you have a particular problem try asking for some help with it and then let it float away. You may find that when you finish your meditation you will have an answer. Do not expect anything earth shattering to happen. Just enjoy doing nothing. This is your spirits time to relax. Enjoy! It's meant to be relaxing—if you get frustrated then you will defeat the object. The more you practise the easier it will be.

Meditation—a first step

When you are comfortable and safe (you are not likely to fall off the chair!) close your eyes and do the protection exercise above. When you have done this, breathe in through your nose to the count of four, hold your breath to the count of four and breathe out to the count of four through your mouth, hold your breath for four and so on. Do this four or five times.

Then imagine you are standing on the edge of a lake. Visualise the lake in front of you. It is dusk. On the other side of the lake you can see the outline of mountains stretching into the evening sky. As you stand there gazing across the lake you feel the first drops of gentle rain on your head. You turn your face to the sky and the rain washes softly over you. It is gentle rain and as it trickles down your upturned face you feel your mood begin to lift. It is a cleansing rain and you stand there enjoying its soothing effect. When you feel ready you turn your back on the lake and begin to walk up the side of the hill. As you walk along the gently climbing path you notice that the light is improving. It is no longer so dark and you feel more energised. All around you are the sounds of scurrying animals but this does not worry you; instead you find it comforting. You can hear your feet crunching on the gravel of the path and you can smell the fragrance of night flowers scenting the air around you. You continue to climb, feeling your mood lift higher with every step.

The sky is now blue and the rain has completely stopped. You can hear the gentle babbling of a stream and as you turn the corner you see the brook in front of you. You step into the brook and let the cool water wash over your bare feet. The sun is now bathing the sky in brilliant light. It is lovely and warm and the water feels cool and refreshing. When you feel ready you continue onwards and upwards eventually coming to a copse of trees. You walk into the glade of trees, enjoying the patterns caused by the dappled sunlight on the ground as it penetrates the branches and leaves of the trees.

One tree in particular takes your eye. You feel drawn to this tree; it may be a sturdy oak, a tall elegant birch, a weeping willow or some other tree. In front of it you can see a blanket and on the blanket there is a particular design. This design is special to you. You go up to it and sit down. The sun is still shining and the air is lively and warm. This is your sacred place and you can go there whenever you choose. While you are sitting there you realise you are not alone. This is not at all frightening but feels wonderfully comforting.

If this is your first time meditating it may well be a relative or someone you know. Otherwise it will be your gatekeeper or a guide (please see Chapter 9 for more information on guides and gatekeepers). Your gatekeeper may well be a relative but could just as easily be someone you haven't met in this life. But your spirit will recognise them. They may speak to you, they may not. You may not feel anything. You may have fallen asleep before you got to this point! It doesn't matter. Meditation is just like anything else. You have to practise. The more you practise the easier it will be. The most important thing is that you shouldn't worry. This is not a race. You will get there in your own time. Just enjoy the peace. Then when you feel ready thank your guides and helpers. Do this even if you have not been aware of anything. They will be there—it is just that you need to practise more to be aware of them! Then get up and retrace your steps back to the lake. When you have reached the lake gradually become aware of your surroundings and the noises from your normal everyday life and open your eyes.

One point to mention is that if you have never meditated before you may find that you cry. This is neither bad nor wrong and nor should it put you off. It is just your spirit's way of cleansing you of all your earthly cares. That's what tears are—our body's way of cleansing ourselves. You will find that if you do cry you will not really feel sad and when you finish you will find you feel wonderfully relaxed and free.

We have stated that it is possible for both science and politics to subscribe to our spiritual framework. This is perhaps more obvious in the theoretical aspects. But the practical elements of our spiritual framework can also be used by both science and politics.

The medical profession has long accepted that meditation is good for you. It lowers your blood pressure and slows your pulse thus giving your heart a chance to recharge. It has long been known that patients who are happy recover quicker. Meditation raises your vibration which allows your spirit "time out." It allows you to clear your mind and thus find solutions to problems that may have seemed insurmountable or to see them in perspective. This reduces your stress levels which again is good for you.

Politically, meditation has long been used by the military of various nations for what is called "remote viewing." Spiritually this is called "projection" and is discussed in more detail in Chapter 10—Spiritual Healing. People were given map co-ordinates to meditate on. They then projected themselves there and reported on what they saw.

"A minute of meditation is a minute of peace and happiness. If meditation is not pleasant for you, you are not practising correctly."
Thich Nhat Hanh—Zen master and poet. (Nominated for the Nobel Peace Prize by Martin Luther King.)

Other religions also include meditation as part of their teachings although they may call it by a different name such as "retreat." There are also spiritual organisations that set aside a specific time every day for all their members to meditate. We understand that the members of Brahma Khumaris meditate for one minute on every hour and are arranging a mass meditation for the autumn of 2007 that is to be televised.

It could also be argued that when we hold two minutes' silence out of respect for those who have died and their families we are also meditating, however briefly.

The next chapter looks at how mediumship can be part of the scientific and political spiritual framework for life.

The rest of this chapter contains alternative meditations. These have been included because we are all different so what is an easy meditation for one person may not be for another.

They are also slightly more advanced in that they direct you to bring back things from your meditation. Don't forget that you should always start your meditation with your protection exercise.

If you would like help in understanding any of the things you have bought back from your meditations please visit the website and email us. We will do our best to answer all enquiries.

Meditation 2

You are sitting in a really comfortable chair looking out onto a beautiful garden. You get up slowly and walk into this beautiful garden. The sun is shining and it is so warm you are just wearing light clothes. Your feet are bare and you can feel the grass between your toes. It is cool and soothing and feels wonderful. You can smell the heady perfumes of sweet peas, jasmine, lavender, roses, and all your favourite flowers mingling together in the air around you. As you walk through the garden you can hear crickets, bees, insects and birds singing, As dragonflies and butterflies flit through the summer haze you feel the warm sun on your skin. All the cares and worries of the day begin to fade away as your senses are filled with all the sights and sounds of a warm summer's day.

You continue your walk through the garden drinking in all these sights and smells and sounds until you reach a small wooden gate. You open the gate and you are in a small winding lane that leads to a wood. Although there are trees you are not cold, just pleasantly cool. The sun is slanting through the branches making patterns on the path in front of you. The path is dry and the few dead leaves crackle under your feet as you walk deeper into the wood. As you continue to walk you are aware of the peace that surrounds you. You can still hear the birds singing and the bees and other insects but the sound is muted now. You gradually identify a new sound; you realise that it is a gentle breeze rustling the upper branches of the trees. The leaves sigh softly as the breeze caresses them and with every step your body feels lighter and your spirits rise as if the breeze is gently blowing your earthly concerns away.

In the distance you see what appears to be a very old tree that is hollow in the middle. Your curiosity aroused you step inside the tree and look around. Although you cannot see any lights you are aware of a warm comforting glow that allows you to see a number of heavy wooden doors. They are all closed and each of them has a number on. You feel yourself drawn to one of these doors. Remember the number as it will be a number that is significant for you. You go towards it and it opens. You step inside and see a table with a monk standing behind it. On the table are a variety of bottles and vessels all different shapes and sizes and colours. One draws your attention and you ask the monk for it. Smiling he pours the liquid of your choice into a goblet of the same colour and hands it to you. You sit down on a comfortable seat in the corner of the room and drink deeply. When you have finished you put the goblet aside to bring back with you and close your eyes.

Now is the time to let your mind wander and let your senses flood with peace, harmony and healing. When you feel it is time to finish, say goodbye to your monk and slowly walk out of the room back into the hollow tree trunk. You have with you your goblet and your significant number and you feel totally at peace. You retrace your steps through the wood and back into the garden.

When you are back in the garden you gradually become aware of all the sights, sounds and smells that surround you. As you step back into your home you become aware of your surroundings, become aware of the chair that you are sitting in and slowly open your eyes. On the piece of paper by your side write down anything you remember including your goblet and significant number.

Meditation 3

You are sitting comfortably in your favourite chair. You are looking out onto a beach. You rise up out of your chair and step onto the beach. It is early evening and the sun is setting in the west—a large orange ball in the sky. The air is warm but not unpleasantly so and your clothes feel loose, flowing and comfortable. You can feel the sand between your toes of your bare feet. It is soft and cool and gently massages your feet as you slowly walk towards the sea.

The waves gently ripple onto the beach, the sound soothing and tranquil. There is a gentle breeze coming off the sea that smells faintly of sun and sand and of the kelp and seaweed that lies on the edge of the waterline. A lone gull shrieks its mournful cry as it circles lazily over the sea to your left. You are walking slowly along the edge of the waterline now. The waves are lapping at your feet making them tingle and you are aware of the sand shrinking round your bare toes as you walk towards the setting sun.

You suddenly become aware of music. It is very faint and comes to you in snatches on the breeze. As you continue your walk you strain your ears in an attempt to identify the music and its location. In front of you there is a cliff that juts out. As you go round it an astonishing sight reaches your eyes. In front of you are rows and rows of brightly coloured tents. In between the tents, linking them together are ribbons of colours that are so bright and pure that you find it difficult to identify them and separate one from another.

As you draw closer you see that there is lady holding out a cloak to you. You take this cloak, noting its colour or colours and pull it round you. As you pull the cloak round you all your problems vanish as if you have become invisible. As you walk amongst the tents you find yourself drawn towards a particular one. It is a particular shape and colour and reminds you of a jewel, stone or crystal. You go inside and sit cross legged on the floor, drawing your cloak round you. Now is the time to let your mind and senses wander and enjoy the sights, sounds and sensations that surround you. When it is time you will come back feeling refreshed and relaxed and full of peace, harmony and love and bringing with you your cloak.

But before you leave your tent look down and you will see either a jewel, stone or crystal. You will bring this back with you. Stand up and leave the tent. Go back to the beach and you will gradually become aware of the sights and sounds of the sea and the waves. As you go back to your chair you will become aware of everyday sights and sounds and slowly open your eyes. Write down anything you remember including the colour or colours of your cloak and the colour of your jewel, stone or crystal.

Meditation 4

You are sitting in a really comfortable chair looking out onto a beautiful garden. You get up slowly and walk into this beautiful garden. The sun is shining and it is so warm you are just wearing light clothes. Your feet are bare and you can feel the grass between your toes. It is cool and soothing and feels wonderful. You can smell the heady perfumes of sweet peas, jasmine, lavender, roses, and all your favourite flowers mingling together in the air around you. As you walk through the garden you can hear crickets, bees, insects and birds singing. As dragonflies and butterflies flit through the summer haze you feel and smell the warm sun on your skin. All the cares and worries of the day begin to fade away as your senses are filled with all the sights and sounds of a warm summer's day.

As you walk through the garden you see a wrought iron gate. You open the gate and go through the gate into the meadow beyond. The meadow slopes down towards a gently flowing stream. At the edge of the water there is a sandy area like a miniature beach. There is a rowing boat resting on the sand with a pair of oars inviting you to climb in. It doesn't matter whether you have ever rowed before or whether you like or don't like boats. Your spirit feels no fear or concern. It knows that you are perfectly safe.

You climb into the boat and begin to row gently downstream. The oars slip softly into the water and the water laps gently at the sides of the boat. After a while you feel sleepy. As you start to feel tired you are suddenly aware that someone else is in the boat with you offering to row. You gratefully hand over the oars and lie back on the seat looking at the brilliant blue cloudless sky above you. The sounds of the gently lapping water merge with the sounds of the countryside and all your fears and worries melt away. Your mind is full of positive thoughts and images. All the negative thoughts and feelings you have held on to for so long are drifting away. You feel free and content and empowered.

You become aware that the boat has moored at a small jetty. You are helped to climb out by your companion. This companion will be with you every time you meditate because they are your gatekeeper. You walk to the end of the jetty and see a large gathering of people. As you grow closer you realise these people are all known to you. These are friends and family who have gone through the veil. They are so pleased to see you that they crowd round you smiling and laughing. Don't worry if you are crying; crying is a necessary part of the healing process and will only happen when you are ready. When it is time you will come back refreshed, at peace, cleansed, healed and empowered.

Say goodbye to your loved ones and ask if there is anything they want you to take back. This will be the first thing that enters your mind, however strange it may seem. You know now that you can go and see them whenever you want. Make your way back to the boat and allow your gatekeeper to take you back. When you reach the meadow you will start to become aware of the sights and sounds of summer. This will become stronger as you walk back through the garden to your chair. In your chair you will become aware of everyday sounds and feelings. Slowly open your eyes and write down anything that you remember, including what you have bought back. If it does not seem relevant to you now it will at the right time.

Chapter 7

Mediumship

"What happens after death is so unspeakably glorious that our imagination and feelings do not suffice to form even an approximate conception of it."

Carl Jung, Psychologist

IN the previous chapter we looked at how to meditate safely and how you can find out the answers for yourselves. We also looked how the political world and the scientific world accept and are already using meditation. This chapter explores the different types of mediumship and the different ways mediums work. It also explains how you can develop your own abilities safely and how science and politics are already part of this spiritual framework.

What is mediumship?

The medium's role is primarily to act as a channel whereby proof of life after life is given. They provide the channel between you and your loved ones, guides and helpers. Like healing, we all have the ability to speak to spirit. We are all spirit anyway so it is just a case of spirit talking to spirit. But we have to learn how to do it safely and how to interpret the messages that we get. We all talk to relatives who have died and invariably we get an answer but we can't always hear it as they answer in many different ways. Mediums also receive messages and communicate with spirit in a variety of ways and it is important that you know the type of medium you are going to or you may be disappointed. There are basically two types of mediumship—spiritual mediumship and psychic mediumship. People often confuse the two. But mediums have many different ways of passing messages to us.

Why are there so many different ways of passing on messages?

The answer to this is quite simple. The reason that there are so many different ways of passing on messages is because we are all different and therefore we all have different abilities and gifts. Mediums will always draw on their own experiences and knowledge in the sense that a medium who is/was a nurse may give quite knowledgeable messages about medical matters. David was in the armed forces so is able to accurately describe uniforms of different regiments and is able to place them in the right historical and geographical context. But even more importantly the people who are benefiting from mediumship are all different. Some people like to see evidence, others like to hear evidence. Some like a very formal medium, others like someone who is more relaxed. Young women like attractive young men and vice versa! For some people proof of life after life is all that is needed, while others like to know something of the direction in which they should be heading. Spirit will never tell you what you should be doing but the help they give will allow you to use your free choice and make your own decisions. Unlike us they can see the whole picture!

What is ESP?

ESP stands for extra-sensory perception. It means acquiring knowledge without using the known senses and can be telepathic, clairvoyant or precognitive.

Psychic mediumship

In everyday language when we say someone is psychic we mean they are able to pick up on other people's thoughts. We have already talked about how powerful our thoughts are. We are all spirit so when we use our psychic ability we are allowing our spirit to communicate with someone else's spirit. We all have this ability but many psychics are able to hone this ability and use it to predict, with varying degrees of accuracy, future events.

Spiritual mediumship

Spiritual mediums, unlike psychic mediums, are communicating with spirits from the realms of Home. In other words they are talking to people who have died. This is possible because it is the body that has died, not the essence of that person that is their spirit. Spiritual mediumship is based on truth and philosophy.

A spiritual medium will give you proof of life after life and when they have given sufficient proof that they are talking to the person they claim to be talking to they may give help and directions that you may choose to follow. The important thing is that they are unlikely to give this message until they have given you proof. This is so you will know that the message you are receiving is from spirit and is not from the medium. A spiritual medium will also give a spiritual address at centres and churches. A spiritual address is when the medium is giving meaningful words that are coming freely from guides in spirit and are philosophical in nature, rather than telling some funny stories about the week they have just had.

Mediums also communicate with spirit in different ways. Some are clairvoyant, others clairaudient or clairsentient but the majority work on a combination of these.

Clairvoyance

Clairvoyance essentially means "clear seeing." The medium sees spirit and the realms of spirit, either as we see each other or as we see pictures on an analogue TV that is not tuned in properly! Spirit will provide the pictures of your loved one's home, garden, property or anything else they want the medium to describe.

Clairaudience

Clairaudience means "clear hearing" and that is exactly what the medium does. They hear spirit either in their mind or physically as we hear each other.

Clairsentience

Clairsentience means "clear sensing" and again that is what the medium does. A medium who is clairsentient will perhaps start by saying that they can smell a particular type of perfume, tobacco, etc and this will be the clue for you that your relative is there.

Psychic Artist

Psychic art is the term used to describe drawing whilst in communication with spirit. Some psychic artists can draw your relative or memories whilst passing on messages from spirit, others will draw images, people, etc whilst in trance or meditation and sometimes in complete darkness. The drawings are the proof that they are in communication with your friend or loved one in the same way as other mediums describe them to you.

Pyschometry

Pyschometry is when the medium holds an item owned by the person they are giving the reading to. It must be something that belongs to the person, preferably something they have had from new. The medium picks up impressions from that article. It helps the medium to focus on the impressions and vibrations that are coming from the object. If you give a medium something that once belonged to someone else and which has been handed down, it will also have their impressions on it. This will result in the medium giving the person who owned the article originally, a reading! In other words, if the article was your mother's the medium may start to describe events, places and memories that were your mother's and mean absolutely nothing to you. As your impressions are also on the item the medium will be giving a mixture of messages and proof, some which is relevant to you and some which is relevant to your mother. The result is confusion for both medium and sitter.

Overshadowing

Overshadowing refers to when a spirit guide "overshadows" a medium or healer. Sometimes the medium or healer will appear to take on the physical characteristics of the guide and/or speak in their voice. Healers are overshadowed by their healing guides but this will be explained more fully in Chapter 9 when we look at healing in more detail.

Trance Mediumship

This is a continuation of the previous point but in trance a medium will not always be fully aware of what they are doing because the spirit guide is using their body to communicate. In trance the medium will give spiritual philosophy or messages in a voice that is not their own. Although they may remember some of what they have said they will not remember all of it. There are many instances of mediums talking in languages that they do not know and have never learnt to speak. Healers are not allowed to give healing in trance unless someone else is with them.

Manifestation

Manifestation refers to when spirit materialises in some form or other. Historically, the most common way they materialised was as ectoplasm. However, this is likely to get less frequent now that we have improved technologically. Digital cameras and digital recording equipment has made it much easier for spirit to provide proof of their existence and as technology advances this will become easier still.

Spiritual Writing

Spiritual writing is the term used to describe writing that is done in either meditation or trance. Spiritual writing will be different from the person's own handwriting and may change several times as different guides and spirits come through. Anyone can do spiritual writing. It is just a case of protecting yourself, meditating and having some paper and a pen to hand so that whilst meditating you can write. Just put the pen on the paper, or let your hand hover freely over the paper, and write whatever comes into your head in the way it comes into your head. Do not worry if it does not seem to make sense when you are writing it. You will find that when you read it back it will make perfect sense. You can use anything to write with that feels comfortable. You do not have to use a pencil. Pens work perfectly. If you look at the Appendix—Spiritual Writings—you can see some examples of spiritual writing. These came through in some of our meditation/development groups. Some were in response to direct questions, others were general messages. They have not been edited in any way and the originals are in a variety of different handwriting although the recipient was just one person.

Inspirational Writing

Inspirational writing also comes from spirit but it is inspired rather than written by spirit. This is just another form of mediumship because the writer is being given spirit philosophy or spirit messages but uses their own abilities and knowledge of a subject to interpret them in a way that people can understand and relate to—like this book.

How do I know it is inspirational writing and not just coming from me?

This is a very good question. Arguably as we are spirit, anything we write comes from spirit! But as a general rule, anything that is positive, uplifting and intended for the good of all comes from spirit. Anything that is negative, intended to wound or hurt probably comes from other places and should be disregarded. Spirit messages are always phrased in a way that is intended to be inclusive of all. Any criticism of existing structures, organisations or people is always meant in a constructive way that will enable them to look for alternative answers and solutions that will change lives for the better.

How do I develop my abilities?

If you would like to develop your talents and abilities you need to find a development group. You can look on our website or at the back of the book for development groups that we can recommend.

How much does it cost to join a development group?

The cost of development groups vary and it would be difficult to give you a price in a book that you may be reading years after it has been written. However, at the time of writing some development groups are free. At the moment we do not charge for our groups. Others start from between £3 an evening and upwards.

What is the difference between closed circles and open circles?

Development groups are often called circles. This is simply because we sit in a circle. We could just as easily sit in a square or a rectangle but then people would be sitting at right angles to each other.

Some circles are closed. This means that they start with a group of people and no one else is normally allowed to come in unless they are screened first. This allows those in the group to progress at a certain pace and to not have to keep going back to the beginning. Our circles have always been open. This means people come and go and it has beginners, those who are more advanced and those in between. We like open circles because it is good to have different energies and makes it easier to learn clairvoyance because with the same people all the time you get to know too much about them This means that when you give clairvoyance you start to wonder whether it is clairvoyance or whether this was something you already knew!

If you join a group and do not feel comfortable do not be put off. It may be that the energies are not right for you and you need to find another circle. It is no-one's fault just a clash of energies and you shouldn't worry. There is a circle that is right for you—you just have to find it!

Are there other types of circles?

Yes. There are trance circles. Usually these are for more experienced people but not always. We all develop at different rates as we do in other areas in our lives. In trance circles the sitters are all overshadowed by their guides and all speak in the meditation. Sometimes the guides will have conversations with each other through the mediums and sometimes they will talk in languages that the mediums do not know or speak normally. (For more about overshadowing please see Chapter 9).

There are also physical circles. In these circles, spirit manifest as ectoplasm. These circles are quite rare now although they used to be quite common. As previously mentioned, advances in technology mean that spirit can make themselves known in other ways so do not need to manifest in this way.

What is a Psychic Supper?

Many centres hold psychic suppers. They are a great evening out. You share a table with five or six other people and a medium. Each person gets a fifteen-minute reading and a fish and chip supper (or some variation on this). You can either book the whole table with your friends or just come and sit with other people. Surprisingly enough you will find that you get on really well with all the other people on the table even if you have never met them before! Most centres arrange it so that you do not know which medium you will get. It is a very inexpensive way of having a more or less private reading for very little money and a chance to socialise with other like-minded people.

We have looked at the different types of mediumship and also at some of the different ways that these mediumistic abilities can be used. In addition we have seen how you can develop your own abilities. In the next chapter we look at some of the most frequently asked questions and explain why visiting a medium or going to a clairvoyant event is interactive. Like most things in life, the more you put in the more you get out. We will explain how you can make the experience better and how you can improve your chances of speaking to those who are in spirit.

But before we do this we would like to have a look at the relationship between mediumship and science and politics.
Scientific knowledge and technology is advancing rapidly. The more scientifically advanced we become the easier it will be for spirit to prove their existence. Science is already picking up the vibrations and by the time you read this there will probably be even more proof. Digital cameras have improved the quality of our photographs and more of us than ever are now able to capture images of spirit and orbs on film. Digital tape recorders are also able to pick up voices of guides when mediums are in trance and their guides are talking through them. This was not possible with older recording devices. Recording equipment is also able to pick up what is called "white noise." These are the noises considered to be made by energy or spirits. It is also increasingly more difficult to cheat!

Professor Peter Fenwick, a neuropsychiatrist at King's College, London is currently leading a research team investigating the phenomena that surrounds death. Around 10% of those who are present at the death of loved ones or who are caring for those who are terminally ill, report strange happenings. Some describe how their relative became more conscious and began having conversations with an invisible presence. Others recall how their loved one suddenly turned to them and reported that another relative was present. Nothing strange in that except that this relative was someone who had died very recently and the person who was terminally ill was unaware of this. Many of the nurses who care for the terminally ill accept that as soon as a patient starts to talk about having a visit from deceased relatives this means that they will soon die. Others report seeing mysterious shapes emerge from the body or lights around the patient. Others talk of a type of phosphorescent light emerging from the body and the most indescribable feeling of peace and love.

Whilst sceptics argue that there is no such thing as the afterlife a more accurate statement would be that, as yet, they have not provided incontrovertible scientific proof. However, because you cannot prove something does not mean that it does not exist. For years there have been scientists who have argued that global warming does not exist despite growing evidence to the contrary. It could also be argued that if mediums have a vested interest in stating that there is an afterlife then sceptics have just as much of a vested interest in maintaining that there is no such thing as life after death. There are almost as many people who earn their living from ridiculing spiritualism as there are who earn their living from it.

What is the relationship between mediumship and politics?

In the last chapter we touched on how the military have used mediums for remote viewing.

Mediumship has been used by the police in many countries to help to find criminals or missing persons. In 2003 psychic Angela McGhee helped police find the killer of 59-year-old landlord Michael Hughes in Walsall. She told police that one of the killers was very close to him. His stepson was subsequently convicted of the murder. There is often reluctance by police to admit to using mediums because they have to work on facts, but if a medium can give them specific details then new lines of enquiries can and have been opened. In this case police have told Angela to "ring them any time!"

There has even been a case where a court in Brazil accepted two letters dictated by a murdered man. In Viamo an unnamed medium claimed the letters were from Ercy da Siva Cardoso who was shot dead three years earlier. The letters were accepted as evidence because the prosecution did not object.

There are also several television programmes from other countries that show how mediums have helped their police.
Police use their instincts all the time. Although some of this comes from their experience much of it comes from listening to the little voice inside their head that tells them someone is guilty even if there does not appear to be supporting evidence.

Whilst they do make mistakes in interpretation, they are often right that the person they are talking to is lying or covering up something, and it might just be something that is unconnected to the investigation.

As well as the police service using mediums there are mediums who are also members of the police force. Some are quite well known to the public.

Chapter 8

Questions Asked About Mediums and Readings

"Be sure that it is not you that is mortal, but only your body. For that man whom your outward form reveals is not yourself; the spirit is the true self, not that physical figure which can be pointed out by your finger."

Cicero

IN the last chapter we said that we would try to answer as many of the most frequently asked questions as we can. The answers to the questions on astrology, organ donation and Alzheimer's can be seen in their original form in the Appendix.

Is there a link between spirit and astrology?

Although at first sight there does not seem to be any link between astrology and spirit, messages from spirit take many forms and astrology can convey spiritual messages. It is our instincts that are our spirit and these that we listen to, even when we think we aren't! Our destinations are also planned even if our route is, to a certain extent, our free choice. If we decide to read our horoscope on a certain day it may well be that we will be given an answer to a question and this may help us to make a decision. This decision to read our horoscope on a certain day in a certain paper, or wherever we decide to look, would have been planned by us in spirit as a pointer to the direction in which we are meant to be going. In this sense it would be no different from suddenly deciding to visit a medium or attend a clairvoyance meeting. However, just as you would not visit a medium every day to find out what you should be doing, trying to read specific messages on a regular basis in a general horoscope that is aimed at millions is pretty unlikely. You are here to experience your life and to make decisions based on your instincts. This means listening to your instincts and making the decisions that feel right to you at that time.

Astrology, like numerology, runes, cards, etc is just another tool. Our lives are planned to begin at a certain times and this includes falling within the influence of certain planets. Not only are we one with everything on the planet, we are also one with everything in the universe. We accept that the moon controls the cycles of the tides and we, our physical bodies, are predominantly water so it is logical that we would also be affected by the cycles of the moon. Thus, those born at certain times will have certain similarities because we are all affected by planetary activity as we are all affected by the cycles of the moon. (Appendix— Saturday August 26, 2006)

Does spirit give us "signs" and if they do, how do we know what are genuine "signs" and what are not?

Signs are often used to provide proof or to guide us in one way or another. Often signs will become apparent after the event. In other words you won't recognise it at the time but you will afterwards or someone else will point it out to you. You also have to remember that as you chose your life you would also have chosen certain signs that would be significant to you at particular times and that may be there to guide you in a certain direction. However, once you arrive on the earth plane you have free will so whether you take any notice is to you. (You should also refrain from seeing signs everywhere! As with anything spiritual or indeed physical, balance is the answer!)

We were looking for a design for the cover of this book. Our original design was very close to another book that we found after Gary had spent ages perfecting it. Although it wasn't exactly the same it was, we felt, too close. In our development groups we usually ask a question. This gives a focus to the meditation and we sometimes get surprising answers. We always ask new members if there is anything they would like to ask and this particular evening the question was about signs and how you could tell etc? The result is the above answer and the cover because one of the answers we got in the meditation included a suggestion for the cover. (For the original reply please see the Appendix)

Is it wrong to ask spirit for help for things that are trivial?

There is a school of thought that says you should not ask spirit for help for trivial things such as looking for a parking place or helping you find your keys! However, as spirit or spirits are with you all the time, they will be delighted if you speak to them regularly. They are your friends and friends are always happy to help, but as with all friendships the balance between giving and receiving should be maintained and always remember to say thank you. They do, however, get fed up if you keep asking them the same question when they have already given you an answer! Wouldn't you? Just because the answer is not what you wanted to hear, repeating the question is not going to give you a different answer.

Is it wrong to grieve the passing of a loved one?

One of the things people are often told is that by continually grieving for their loved one they are preventing them from progressing spiritually. Whilst it is not good to continually grieve for someone because it means you are not getting on with your life, grieving is a normal reaction. You need to grieve to be able to move on and crying is a way of cleansing yourself. Obviously it would upset your loved one to see you unhappy but if you did not grieve at all it would be very unnatural. There is no set time for grieving; everybody is different.

But perhaps one way of thinking about it would be to put yourself in your loved ones shoes (so to speak). If it was you who had died would you really want the person that you loved to spend the rest of their life in mourning? Wouldn't you like to see them looking after them selves and moving on? This doesn't mean that you shouldn't talk to them. You can do that whenever you like. But tell them the good things as well as the bad, the funny as well as the sad. When they were here you didn't only speak to them when you were miserable you shared the joys of your life as well. Just because they are no longer physically with you doesn't mean they can't share in the happy times as well as the sad times. Finding happy things to talk about will also help you because to talk about happy things you have to feel them, which means getting on with your life.

One final point is that if you are totally engrossed in your grief you may miss the signs that they are still with you. Grief and sadness can be a negative emotion and as spirits work on the light they find it more difficult to come through barriers of negative emotion.

Why do some mediums use tarot cards, runes or angel cards?

Some mediums use visual aids to help them concentrate and interpret better. Also some people like to feel more involved in the process of having a reading. By shuffling the cards and choosing particular cards, runes etc they feel the reading is more personal.

Can anyone use tarot cards to give readings?

Yes. You can buy books on how to interpret tarot cards but it is not a game: you are still trying to communicate with spirit. If you try to communicate with spirit without using protection you could invite spirits that you do not want to talk to. If you would like to learn how to communicate with spirit safely it is probably best to join a development group.

It is also a fallacy that you have to be given tarot or any other cards rather than buy them yourself. If, after learning how to communicate safely, you wish to have tarot cards it is much better to buy them yourself. This way you will know which set are the right ones for you and they will not have anything attached to them because they are new. If you are given cards of any description you should always cleanse them before use. If you are a novice it is best to ask someone more experienced to cleanse them for you.

Can children see spirit?

Yes, children can see spirit. In fact they are more likely to see spirit than adults. There are three reasons for this. The first is that they are nearer to spirit because they have not been on the earth plane long. Secondly, they are also purer in spirit because they have not been as corrupted by the vibrations of the earth plane. Thirdly, no one has told them they can't see spirit! To them it is perfectly normal because they have an open mind.

However, there are dangers in this. The fact that they are pure and have an open mind leaves them particularly vulnerable to black spirits and negative thought forms as well as the negative vibrations of the earth plane. If your child is seeing spirit do not panic. Talk to them about who they are seeing in a way that does not scare them. The majority of the time there is absolutely no problem and the people they see are usually relatives. You can use your own white light to protect them as a precaution at night when they go to sleep and when they are old enough you can teach them to use the white light themselves. This is the spiritual equivalent of telling them not to talk to strangers. It also helps to prevent nightmares. However, if you have any concerns and you feel you child maybe seeing black spirits or attracting negative thought forms or you just feel unsure and out of your depth then please contact one of the organisations mentioned at the back of this book. We have suggested the organisations at the back of this book because we know they have experience in dealing with this kind of enquiry. Unfortunately there are people, as in all walks of life, who will try to help without knowing what they are doing.

Why are messages obscure?

There are many reasons for this. When your mum rings you she usually says "hello it's me"—she doesn't say "hello it's your mother from 123 Acacia Gardens West London post code ABC 123!" We are also so sceptical that if they say the obvious we will assume the medium has some inside knowledge of our lives—they do but not of the earthly physical variety! We also have preconceived ideas of who we are expecting to come through. It may not be possible for a loved one to come through because they may still be receiving healing. There is no time at Home so what may seem an age to us is but a blink of time at Home.

We have awful memories and don't always remember everyone we have ever met. When we go back to spirit we are able to re evaluate our lives so we are able to see all the people whose lives have touched our own. It may be that you have had a really positive, life-changing effect on someone and not even known it. That person, once in spirit, may choose to come back and thank you. Also, the more obscure the person, the less likely you are to believe the medium has had help and the more likely you are to believe the message you are being given.

Often the message is personal and it is not necessary for the medium to know the circumstances. Mediums give messages to many people and are unlikely to remember the messages they give but you may not really want a stranger to know your private business so the medium is given enough so that they can communicate the message in a way that you will understand but not enough for him/her to understand.

Another reason messages may be obscure is because it is very important that the medium does not push you in a certain direction. If, for instance, you are going to become a famous medium (!), it is important that you go towards that goal in the way that you are meant. If you are told that before you are ready you may make choices that will put you on a different path, you may meet different people and have different influences. This could all affect the outcome.

The more readings you have the more obscure the messages are likely to be because they are giving you the opportunity to do some research i.e. ask relatives, which will also have the effect of providing proof to them.

Sometimes you are given messages that seem to be obscure to you but this is because they are meant for your partner, family or friends. By discussing your messages with your family and friends you may find that they will be able to take some of the messages that you have found obscure.

Finally, most mediums will tell you that spirit will normally give you the answer three times. However, if you keep having readings and asking the same question, they will get fed up giving you the same answer! After all, if someone kept asking you the same question wouldn't you get fed up?

Why do spirits sometimes not come through clearly?

The person who is coming through will come through in such a way that you will recognise them. If they are timid in life they will not come through bold and assertive because you would not know who they were when the medium described them to you. It may also be the first time they have come through so they may be really nervous, excited, emotional, and in a hurry to say as much as possible. This may make it difficult for the medium to understand what they are saying.

Also it helps if you answer when the medium is giving you a message. It is a conversation and your voice helps to make the contact stronger. You wouldn't sit in silence if you were speaking on the phone. You do not need to give the medium loads of information but a "yes" or "no" is really important.

The message is coming through from another vibration thus it can easily be distorted as it passes from one medium to another (no pun intended!). Therefore, just as when you put a stick in water the effect of refraction is to make the stick look like it is distorted, the message is not as clear as it would be if you were talking to someone in the same room.

Why do some people not get messages?

There are many reasons why people do not get messages. Let's first look at why people do not get messages in a public arena.

Although people sitting in the audience have presumably come in the hope of getting a message many do not actually want one. When the medium looks round they are saying inwardly "please don't come to me"! This lowers their vibration so that in an audience their light or energy is too dull to be picked out. The medium will be directed to the brighter lights within the audience. Another reason could be that because their relatives are not used to coming through they find it difficult so a public arena may not be the best place to come through for the first time.

In a private sitting people will still often block the messages. People go to mediums with preconceived ideas as to who is going to come through. This means they are not receptive to anyone else who is not the person they are expecting. There are so many people in spirit who wish to talk to us we need to be much more open and accept the messages much more readily even if we can't immediately place the person who is giving it. Whilst we are busy trying to work out who it is we have missed half the message!

The reason it may not be the person we are expecting is that when we die we are first welcomed by our relatives and friends. Once they have welcomed us and we have caught up on all the gossip we feel reassured and are then ready to go to the halls of healing to cleanse ourselves of our earthly lives. This may take some time and some relatives may not be able to come through in this lifetime because they are still receiving healing. This is one of the reasons that giving healing to people who are terminally ill is so helpful. It reduces the amount of time that they will need healing in spirit.

Some people who have not had messages before will also be quite frustrated and anxious and again this communicates itself to spirit. Frustration and anxiety are negative emotions and spirits of light do not work on these vibrations. For them to come through there needs to be vibrations of love and light. That is often why there is laughter at these sittings and evenings. Laughter raises the vibrations.

There are also people who are not working and living their lives on the vibration of love and light and are actively working on an altogether darker vibration. They, accordingly, will not receive messages from mediums who work on the vibration of light.

Other people are not prepared to believe and are so sceptical that they would not accept anything as proof however strong that proof is. By continually denying the messages and refusing to accept anything they are effectively putting up a barrier. This will communicate itself to their relatives who will then not come through. This can be very distressing and frustrating for these spirits who are watching the person on the earth plane and would like to offer guidance and some words of help or comfort, but are unable to because the person is essentially blocking this contact. This is not to say that you should just believe everything, but you do need to be open and think about it and how it might relate to your life.

Sometimes people are not ready to accept the messages from spirit. It is just not the right time or it is not in their pathway at present. If you genuinely wish to have contact with your relatives and none of the above seems to apply then have some healing and see if that makes a difference. But you must be honest with yourself!

One way to improve the reception and clarity of the messages when going either to a public evening of clairvoyance or a private sitting is to use your white light. This will raise your vibration and make the contact much clearer. It is a conversation between you and your relative. The medium is just a channel between you. If you were having a telephone conversation you would not just sit there and say nothing! If you were having a face to face conversation with a relative would you sit there with an expression on your face that said quite clearly that you were not interested in hearing anything they had to say? If you did, would they talk to you?

Another point to bear in mind is that during the second world war because of the movement of troops and other changing social factors people did not always know who their biological father was. This is going to become increasingly more common because of the way our lives are now structured. If parents split up very early on in a child's life and the child loses contact with the absent parent it is also going to be harder for people to find out their family history.

Finally, when asked this question in our development circle one of the guides said jokingly that people should be pleased they weren't getting messages because it meant they weren't getting nagged anymore!

Why do children who are in spirit sometimes come through at different ages from that at which they may have died?

It may be that they died as babies in which case they would not be able to communicate with you, so they project themselves at another age that allows you to see them as you would like to—perhaps as a young child dancing or playing football.

It may also be that there was an age at which they and you were really happy or had special memories for you or at an age before they were ill.

Will a medium say anything that is likely to embarrass me in a public arena?

No, they shouldn't. Spirit will always give information in a way that is respectful and will never give any information that could embarrass you in any way. If a medium does say something deliberately to embarrass you it is coming from him or her and not from spirit. Spirit wishes you to communicate with them. If they embarrass you there is a fair chance you will not come back again and they will not have an opportunity to speak to you again.

Can a medium read my mind?

No more than anyone else can! They may pick up on thoughts or body language because we all do that but a medium is not working on this vibration. They tune in so that they are communicating with spirits from Home. They do not need to read your mind.

Will a medium tell me if something bad is going to happen?

No. A proper medium will never tell you if something bad is going to happen. Most mediums are not given this information. If a medium does tell you something bad is going to happen they are not a proper medium or they are not working in the light!

Will a medium tells me something is definitely going to happen?

No. You have free choice and free will. A medium is there to pass on a message. If you do not like that message then you have the free will to do something about it. Maybe that is why you are given that message in the first place. On the other hand if it is something you wish to happen you should be wary of changing your life in ways you would not normally consider or you may miss the opportunity altogether. Example like: "you will meet a tall dark handsome stranger," so you sit at home waiting for the phone to ring and miss the opportunity to meet him because he was at your local supermarket! Or you are told you will do well in your exams so you stop studying!

Chapter 9

Questions Asked About Spirituality In General

"Choose rather to be strong of soul than strong of body."

Pythagoras

What is a séance?

A séance is when people gather together to contact the spirits of those who have died. This may sound similar to a development group, meditation circle or clairvoyant evening and although that is true to a certain extent there are subtle differences. The word seance, like the word religion, has unpleasant connotations that derive from its historical origins. Throughout history anything to do with Spiritualism has been demonised by religions, particularly Christianity. This has led to its depiction in films, books, etc as either something to be feared, trivialised or treated as fraudulent. Because of this the word seance is enough to put most people off anything to do with Spiritualism, which, of course, was the intention. Add to this the seances that are carried out by people who have no idea what they are doing, by those whose intentions are less than pure and it is easy to see why seances have become synonymous with danger and fear. However, anything can be dangerous if you do not know what you are doing, and the point of joining a development group or meditation circle is for you to learn how to communicate with spirit safely.

Are Ouija boards dangerous?

Yes. They are extremely dangerous if you do not know what you are doing. Would you go parachuting without learning first? No. Communicating with spirit, if you do not know what you are doing, is like jumping out of an aeroplane with a parachute without having lessons! You have no idea what is going to happen. If you are trying to communicate with spirit you need to make sure the spirits you are attracting are those of the light. We would not suggest anybody uses an Ouija board even with protection. They are not toys. We are not trying to frighten you but too many people treat speaking to spirit as a game and attract negative spirits to them. This also applies to so-called "angel boards" which are just another name for Ouija boards.

What is an exorcism?

We have talked about how dangerous it is to try and communicate with spirit without protection. The following are the reasons why.

You may attract spirits or energies who are trapped within the earth plane and who do not wish to go to the light. These can take different forms.

There are thought forms that attach themselves to your aura. People who have attachments are usually prone to all the negative thoughts and emotions. They may have good ideas but rarely put them into practice because of the little voice inside them that tells them it is a waste of time and lists all the things that could go wrong. This lack of ambition and purpose is a result of the negative thought form that has attached itself to the person. These thought forms often delight in causing trouble to the person they are attached to and anyone who comes into their sphere. People who have thought forms attached to them often live very miserable existences. They usually seem to everyone else to be on a permanent crash course to disaster.

The energy or spirits may be more than negative—they may be malevolent. They may "tell" the person they are attached to that violence is the answer. These are "black" spirits. Young people are particularly vulnerable because they are much more open and receptive to spirit than older people. Others who are vulnerable include those who get involved in any type of paranormal or spiritual activity without first protecting themselves and without knowing what they are doing, and those who are aware that they have a psychic ability but refuse to acknowledge it. If it is there it will not go away if you ignore it. All that will happen is that you will be seeing and attracting negative thought forms and black spirits. If this applies to you use your protection whenever you feel uncomfortable and before you go to sleep at night and seek professional advice. (See Chapter 12 for details of some useful contacts or our website).

Another danger is that you will attract a malevolent spirit to your property. There are numerous examples of poltergeist activity and properties where there appears to be malevolent paranormal activity.

Exorcism is the name given to the removal of these attachments and malevolent spirits. All religions believe in and carry out exorcisms. Do not attempt to carry out an exorcism if you do not know what you are doing. Do not attempt to speak to or communicate with these attachments, thought forms or malevolent spirits in any way.

In this case a little knowledge is a very dangerous thing. If you have any concerns about someone you know or about yourself then please contact someone who has experience in this area.

Science is often able to pick up paranormal activity through the use of technology and this can be used to prove its existence but it is not a good idea to ask "ghost hunters" in to see what they "pick up" unless they are also experts in the field of exorcism and psychic rescue.

From a political point of view we have only to turn on the news to see examples of all of the above. It is also possible that some people who are diagnosed with depression, paranoia and other psychiatric illnesses may be particularly sensitive to other vibrations. Some of those who are prescribed anti-depressants may be picking up on the negative energies, vibrations and thoughts around them rather than actually suffering from a psychiatric illness. We are NOT suggesting you stop taking prescribed medication without the advice of your doctor or consultant. We are just suggesting a possible alternative reason for the condition which the medical profession may wish to consider. Of course seeing, hearing and feeling and acting on negative voices, thoughts and vibrations could also be a sign of a psychiatric illness, so each case should be looked at on an individual basis.

What are Indigo and Crystal children?

There has been much talk of "Indigo" and "Crystal" children in recent months and even television programmes devoted to the subject. The following is a summary. There are several books and websites dedicated to this topic, with further information if you wish to explore in more detail.

Indigo children have been here for the last hundred years and a significant number were born after the second world war. But in the 1970s large numbers were born. Thus there are many people in their twenties and thirties who are Indigos. Indigo children are essentially here to rid the world of governments, education and legal systems that lack integrity; therefore they have warrior spirits, fiery tempers and determination. Proponents of Indigo children believe that it is these characteristics that have led to them being diagnosed with ADHD and ADD by those who value conformity and resist change. Because their role is to usher us into a new world of integrity and honesty their inner lie detectors are an integral part of them, allowing them to know when they are being lied to or manipulated. In the world which Indigos are ushering in, intuition and feelings are more acceptable and communication will be quicker because more people will be developing their psychic and spiritual abilities.

Thus Crystal children, who are those born after 2000, are incredibly telepathic, meaning many do not speak until they are three or four years old. This leads to diagnoses of autism.

In contrast to Indigos, Crystal children are blissful, even-tempered, have eyes that are penetrating and wise beyond their years and are fascinated with rocks and crystals. Despite late speech development, Crystal children are communicative, caring and philosophical and spiritually gifted.

Both Indigo and Crystal children are very sensitive and psychic. These names were given to the children because it most accurately describes the colours and energy patterns of their auras.

89

There are also Indigo and Crystal adults who are composed of two groups. Firstly there are those who were born Indigos and are now making the transition to Crystal. The second are those born without these qualities but who are making the transition through hard work and their own spiritual awakening.

Proponents of these views believe that these children are a new species of human, here to help us all make the transition to our next stage of evolution.

What is the difference between angels, ghosts, gatekeepers and guides?

"Angels can fly because they take themselves so lightly."

New Age saying

These are four different levels. When we asked this question in one of our meditation groups, we were told that angels are really there to protect you from passing to spirit at the wrong time and as one of our guides remarked, "Angels don't say a lot!"

On a more serious note though, gatekeepers are there to protect us from negative energies. However, spirits, like us, are all at different levels. They are also evolving and progressing. If a gatekeeper is only at a certain level they may not always recognise more powerful negative energies, which is why we have to learn to protect ourselves. The stronger we become the stronger our gatekeepers will also become.

Guides are spirits of different levels who come through to us to answer our questions. We will have many guides throughout our lifetime as the more we progress the higher the guides that we will communicate with. We also have healing guides who overshadow healers.

Ghosts are spirits who are trapped on the earth plane. They can be people who have died so suddenly that they cannot accept they have died or people who are so attached to their physical body or other physical things that they cannot let go.

There are also occasions when an event is so traumatic that it leaves an impression in the place where it happened. These vibrations are often picked up by mediums and psychics.

What is cleansing?

A medium will go into a property and rid it of the negative vibrations within and replace these with positive vibrations. This can sometimes result in a psychic rescue.

What is psychic rescue?

Psychic rescue usually refers to a medium helping a spirit that is trapped in the earth plane to return home. The medium communicates with the spirit who is usually quite distressed and explains to them that their loved ones are waiting and it is time to go to the light. It can also be used to describe the exorcism of black spirits.

What is an out-of-body experience?

An out-of-body experience is when a person is able to see and hear real things and events that are happening in another location without physically being there. These experiences appear to be quite common with an estimated one-in-ten to one-in-twenty people having experienced this at least once. Most of these experiences seem to happen when people are relaxed—either asleep, dreaming or just resting. The most common or well-documented type of out-of-body experience are those that happen to people who "have died." Most of these describe looking down on their bodies whilst people are trying to revive them. They accurately describe the events and people present although, to all intents and purposes, they are physically dead.

What is a near-death experience?

This is a continuation of the last point where the physical body has apparently died. In this case the person describes going through a tunnel towards a beautiful light. They experience no fear, only joy, and see many of their relatives waiting for them but are told that it is not their time. They then find themselves back in their body as their physical body begins to live again. Many people who have experienced this say that it changes their whole perception of life and they no longer have a fear of dying.

What is astral projection?

Astral projection is when the astral body separates from the physical body and travels without it. This normally happens in sleep. In an untrained person this travel is often vague and formless with the memory retaining very little. However, it is possible to control the astral body to travel long distances and even to project it at will. There is plenty of information on the internet and many books are available that explain this in more detail.

If someone has Alzheimer's is it possible to communicate with their spirit?

This is one of the questions that we asked spirit for some help with and the original answer is in the Appendix (Sunday August 27, 2006). Because Alzheimer's is a physical disease that affects the physical body there is nothing to prevent communication with the spirit of the person afflicted. Communicating with spirit on this plane is done at a psychic level rather than the spiritual level usually associated with a medium talking to the spirit of someone who has died. The biggest problem would probably be with acceptance that this communication is genuine. Although the spirit of the person could provide information that only they would know, it could be argued that those in spirit would also have this information. However, wherever the proof comes from, it would appear to be a good thing for those with Alzheimer's to be able to communicate.

If an organ is donated will the spirit go with it?

No. The spirit is attached to a physical body. When the body dies the silver chord that attaches it to the body is cut and the spirit returns home. The body is a physical entity and is the sum of its parts. In other words each part of the body is also a physical entity. If you decide to donate an organ after your death you are practising unconditional love because you are giving someone else the chance of life. Who knows how important that life may turn out to be?

There are rare cases where it has appeared the recipient may have taken on some of the characteristics of the donor. The physical body and all its components bear the imprint of the spiritual essence of the person rather like an item does that a medium would use in pyschometry. When we donate an organ a vibration from our spirit will go with it. This is because we are mind, body and spirit and the three are interconnected and intertwined and the imprint of spirit is in all. Yes, this does include the blood but the blood is quickly diluted so does not bear this impression for long. But this does not mean that the personality of the person is also passed on. Only the part of the personality that is the spiritual essence of the person is passed on. How long this imprint or vibration stays with the recipient depends on the number of parts that are received and also on the organ function itself. The new organs are absorbed into the spirit of the recipient and eventually become a part of the spirit of that person. Discussions on BBC Essex with a man who had received a heart and lung transplant bear this out. He received these transplants because of cystic fibrosis. However, his heart was healthy so was given to another man. By chance (!) the two men met and became friends. Both were interviewed on the programme. When asked by the interviewer if the recipient had taken on characteristics of the donor the recipient said that he had not. There was no psychic or spiritual link between them. The only connection was their friendship. (Appendix—July 2006)

What is cryogenics?

Cryogenics is when someone has their body frozen after death in the hope that in the future there will be a cure for the condition that killed them. They hope that future technology will be able to revive the body and cure the condition and they will be able to continue their life. How would this work from a spiritual point of view? It would seem to be something of a spiritual minefield!

The spirit leaves the body at the moment of death. It may take another 100 or 200 years for the technology to be able to revive a body, if ever. But let's just assume it is possible. The original spirit may have taken another life by then and be living that life. It may not be in their spiritual pathway to re-take the same body. On the other hand, if the original spirit re-takes the same body it means they have to wait until that body has been revived. They may have lived another life in the meantime and evolved to another level. What happens in that case? Maybe another spirit will take this body. In any case why would you want to keep the same body when you could have the choice of a new one?

There is a difference between this and someone who suffers a heart attack and is resuscitated or someone who drowns in temperatures that are so low it is possible to revive them without brain damage occurring. In these cases the spirit has not left the body because it knows the body will survive. It is just part of that spirit's pathway. Reviving a body after several years or decades could be considered to be "playing God." Maybe this is something that should be considered carefully. However, as we have said, we do not have all the answers and any thoughts on this would be welcome!

Do animals have individual spirits?

No. Animals are part of a group spirit. But if an animal is "personalised" (i.e. it develops an almost human-like personality) it may be that they can cross from a group soul to an individual soul.

Could I choose to be an animal in my next life?

No. You take lives to evolve. You cannot "evolve" backwards because you would not be evolving.

When does the spirit enter the physical body?

The spirit enters the physical body at the moment the umbilical chord is cut. Until then the baby is a physical entity only and is part

94

of the mother. Once the umbilical chord is cut the baby takes on an individual existence and therefore needs an individual spirit.

What happens when we miscarry?

One of the most common misconceptions is that if we miscarry our baby will go back to spirit and grow up there. As we said in Chapter 2 we, as spirits, choose our lives to experience certain things and these experiences help us to evolve. Unfortunately it is through pain that we evolve most of all because it is the experience of pain that makes us strong. There would be no point in a spirit choosing a life that was not going to happen. There would be no experience to have. The experience is for the mother, father, friends and family. An experience they, as spirits, have chosen. This may come as a shock to many people but it is not intended to trivialise or in any way belittle this terrible experience—just to explain it. Many women feel guilty as if there was something they could have done to prevent it happening. They could not—it was always meant to happen. For whatever reason, they as spirit have chosen to have that experience.

If someone commits suicide will they go to hell?

No. Remember we have chosen this life to have a specific range of experiences. These experiences are agreed with the other spirits who are going to be our family, loved ones, etc. If someone commits suicide it is because they and those around them have chosen this experience in this life. It is for us to learn from our experiences and to grow stronger. Again this is not meant to trivialise such a terrible experience but to try and explain it in a spiritual way.

In times of despair we often feel that our life is a waste of time. This is not the case. No life is ever wasted. Apart from our spiritual evolution our physical existence is also never wasted. We do not live our lives in isolation. Throughout our life we are continually interacting with other people and we never know whether something we may have said or done has changed some one else's life. In other words we are like cogs in a giant spiritual machine that is constantly turning and touching other cogs. And like all machines the cogs can turn either way.

We have already explained how we, as spirits, choose our lives. These lives are carefully planned. Although we may not always be able to see how our interaction with others can affect their lives we should always bear this in mind. A simple smile or kind word can change someone else's life for the better. The opposite is also true. A careless word can often wound and cause untold damage to someone if they are already feeling low.

If we have many lives, are they connected?

Only in the sense that once you have had certain experiences and have learnt from them you would not need to have then again. You cannot always understand some of the strange ways people act because you have evolved past that stage. The lives as such are not connected and you will not remember them here unless it is in your pathway to remember them. If it is in your pathway you may wish to revisit previous lives through past life regression.

What is past life regression?

Past life regression is when you open your memory box and project yourself back into a past life. As spirit we all have memory boxes which contain all the records of our past lives. These are sealed whilst we are here because we do not need to have them open. Do not attempt past life regression unless you know what you are doing or you are with someone who knows what they are doing. You will see the life your spirit led before and you will see how you died which may not be very nice, and the results of this could be very damaging. However, if it is done properly, past life regression can be very interesting although it is not necessary to see past lives to improve your present life.

Is there such a thing as karma?

Not if you mean can some specific act done in a previous life affect your prospects in this life. The two lives are unconnected in that sense. However, as spirit you take lives to experience things. Take this example: You have experienced something horrible in one life—maybe you killed someone in a jealous rage and then realised that what you had done was terrible. You might choose to come back in another life and experience that jealous rage again to see if you had learned to handle it better. Alternatively, in your next life, you might be totally appalled by the jealousy of others because you have experienced its destructive power and know it is something that should be let go.

Having said that, you cannot spend your life trying to hurt people without some of it coming back to you. Remember what we said about thoughts and how powerful they are. Take this example: If you continually lie and manipulate your partner to control them, because you are frightened they will leave you—they will eventually see through you and do exactly that. Not only are you sending out all the wrong thoughts saying this is what you want to happen—you are also using your gift of love in a negative way. Eventually you will be on your own—something that your own actions have led to. Perhaps this could be described as karma.

Are we judged when we die?

No. Not in the sense that we would normally mean by "judged." We are here to learn. Learning, by its very nature, means making mistakes. If we did not make mistakes we would already be perfect and we would not need to be here! When we die we assess our lives and see what we have learnt, where we could have done better and where, quite frankly, we have made a mess of it! But it is an assessment, not a judgement.

If we have not done very well we can always come back and repeat the same experiences!

Why do we sometimes seem to keep repeating the same experiences?

We will often find that the same situation will arise more than once in this lifetime. Although we think we have had this experience

97

and don't need it again there may be a good reason for this. Perhaps it just needs reinforcing or the situation is a variation on the original so needs a slightly different approach. It may be that we have not recognised that it is the same experience until it is too late to stop or we are going to use that experience in a positive way to help others so need to experience all its variations.

A perfect example of this is an abusive relationship. Victims of abusive relationships—both women and men—invariably walk into one abusive situation after another. The reasons behind this are quite complicated and would take too much space to explain in detail. Briefly abusive relations happen because of the insecurities of the abuser. They are generally very weak and are attracted to people who appear weaker than themselves. These are usually people who are vulnerable at that time. Generally they are not weak people but very strong. It is both the strength and the vulnerability that attracts the abuser. The vulnerability attracts them because they need to feel needed and vulnerable people are easier to control. But the strength also attracts them because they want to use this strength for their own purposes. Abusers invariably get their victim to do things they do not have the courage to do themselves. These do not have to be illegal although they frequently are. Sometimes it is just as simple as getting the victim to deal with any aspect of officialdom that they don't want to deal with. Abusers are invariably very plausible and always have good reasons why they can't do things themselves. By manipulating their victim into dealing with situations they themselves are frightened of they gradually build up the confidence of the victim.

However, that confidence eventually becomes a threat. It becomes a constant juggling act between building up or destroying the victim's confidence. Because abusers are insecure they need someone to need them. They also do not think that anyone could love them therefore you must be deceiving them. Because they usually lie they assume their partner must be lying too. They then set out to control their partner or friend because they don't trust them.

This becomes a cycle of abuse because the victim loses self-confidence and believes the abuse is their fault. The abuser is constantly sending out thought messages that his/her partner/ friend is going to leave them for someone else and eventually this becomes reality. Unfortunately the person the victim is attracted to is attracted to the victim because they are vulnerable. The cycle then begins again and is reinforced when there are children involved because they learn the same behaviour patterns.

The only way to break this cycle is for the victim to live on his/her own for a while to heal themselves. Once they have dealt with the emotional problems caused by this they will become different people, and once this happens they will not be attracted to the same type of people nor will they be attractive to the same type of people.

When I die am I likely to meet all my ex's?

Only if they are at the same level of evolution as you are and only if you choose to.

When you die your spirit returns Home and after the healing and assessment time you will continue to learn and evolve but you will be with spirits who are on the same level as you. They may be at slightly different stages on that level but this is so you can all help each other.

Do we all go Home when we die?

That depends on how you have lived your life. We have explained that it is a scientific fact that everything has an opposite and therefore if there is light there must be dark. If you have lived your life trying to harm others physically, emotionally, sexually or any other way and this is a deliberate conscious decision on your part you are not living your life in the light. You are consciously choosing a path that will lead you to evolve further towards the dark. When you die you will go to a place that is the opposite of Home.

This is a very complicated question and would take up considerable space to explain properly. This book is just an introduction to life. If we make it too long people may be put off and will not read to the end! Rather than gloss over it or try to give a short answer we will cover it more comprehensively in future books. The only thing we would like to add is that everything needs to be in balance and at the moment the planet is more dark than light. Whether that changes is up to us. The more the dark is influenced by the light the less extreme the light has to be. One way of redressing the balance is to learn how to heal, not only ourselves but our planet.

Chapter 10

Healing

"The body, being the temple of the living spirit, should be carefully tended in order to make it a perfect instrument."
Swami Vishnu—Devananda

WE have seen how science can prove mediumship and how politically mediumship can be used for the good of the community, saving money and resources. The same can be said of healing as we shall see.

Spiritual healing

There are lots of myths about spiritual healing and lots of mumbo jumbo about who can give healing and how you should do it. It is perfectly true that anyone can be a healer—they just have to choose to do it. But there are lots of different types of healers and there are many reasons people choose to be healers. There are also a lot of so-called healing therapies that are essentially spiritual healing with a fancy name. There are several reasons for this. People can be put off by the term "spiritual." People are also suspicious of something that doesn't cost anything. But the most common reason is that it allows high prices to be charged for something that spiritual healers provide freely. For some reason we all feel that if we pay large amounts of money for something it will work better. Maybe we should remember the saying "the best things in life are free!"

What is spiritual healing?

Spiritual healing, or natural healing as it is sometimes called, gives healing to our spirit and this re-energising of our spiritual self helps our physical body to heal itself. Physically, our bodies have their own store of pain-relieving hormones, and healing works by tapping into these stores and allowing them to be released into the body. However, if you think about it, healing can be as simple as smiling at someone. We all give healing every day when we listen to someone's problems, when we offer help, when we make people laugh, when we talk to people in a positive way. In this sense everyone can be a spiritual healer and these ways of healing are no less important than what we shall call the "hands on" type of spiritual healing that we will explain next.

So what is "the hands on" or contact type of spiritual healing?

First of all you do not need to put your hands on anybody to give them healing. We have only used this term to try and separate it from all the other types of practical healing we have just mentioned. This type of spiritual healing involves acting as a channel for healing energy to flow through you from spirit to the person you are giving healing to. Yes, we know that sounds really complicated but it isn't really and you don't need to understand it to give this type of healing to your family. You can give healing to your family whenever you want and we shall explain how in a minute, but if you want to give healing to the general public you have to take a recognised course with a recognised organisation and pass an assessment. This is to protect the public from people who may want to charge huge amounts of money, guarantee cures and generally abuse their gift. A certificated healer rarely charges and never guarantees cures.

What is absent healing and can anybody do it?

The simple answer to this is yes. We can all do absent healing. There are five main ways that you can do absent healing.

The first is through what we know as prayer. All you need to do is ask that the person you are concerned about receives healing. Use your own words but remember we are here to experience certain things so it may not be part of that person's pathway to be cured. However, asking for healing for them will help give them the strength to deal with their problem or reduce the level of pain and suffering. It does not have to be a physical problem. We all need healing to a certain degree and emotional problems are just as damaging as physical ones. The most important thing is that you mean it!

The second way is through projection. Yes, we know that sounds a bit complicated but it isn't really. The chapter ends by explaining how you can give healing to a member of your family or a friend. You just use the same technique except you are visualising yourself as being with the person who needs healing. In other words you get comfortable, protect yourself with the white light and then imagine you are with the person and just follow the instructions for giving healing to a family member.

The third way is by an article or object. This is a good way to give healing to someone you have never met. If you have an article that belongs to that person or a photograph of them you can sit comfortably, protect yourself with the white light and then ask that healing goes to the person whose article or photograph you have.

The fourth way is to put the names of anybody you hear of who needs healing in a book and then sit comfortably, protect yourself with the white light and then ask for healing for everybody in the book. Many healers, churches and spiritual centres have these books and will always add names to them if you ask.

The fifth way is by sitting in a group and you all send healing to the person who needs it. If you sit in a development group or you are meditating you will do this as part of the meditation (See Chapter 7). There are several groups around the world which hold group healing sessions for their members and others, like The Harry Edwards Healing Sanctuary that hold a "healing minute" every night at 10pm. As many people as possible are encouraged to join in, wherever they may be in the world.

We can all do this. You do not need to have training, certificates or anything else, just the genuine desire to help other people. You don't even need to take time out of your busy life—you can do it when you get into bed at night before you go to sleep.

Don't worry if you fall asleep; the healing will go where you have asked.

Absent healing is just as effective as contact healing and unlike contact healing everyone is able to do it.

Do you have to be special to be a healer?

No, definitely not. As we have just said we all have the ability to heal others just as we all have the ability to hurt others. So whether you choose to hurt others or heal them is really up to you. Remember the gifts we all have and the free choice we have in how we use them?

What is the difference between giving healing to a person and giving healing to an animal?

The main difference is that animals, unlike humans, exist by using their sensitivity and vibratory field. If they do not like your vibrations they will not let you near them.

However there are strict regulations that govern giving healing to animals. Only a qualified veterinary surgeon may diagnose illnesses and ailments in animals and only a veterinary surgeon can give advice that is based on those diagnoses.

Can anyone receive spiritual healing?

Yes. You do not have to believe in anything for the healing to work. It is not "faith" healing. We are all spirit and spiritual healing works on the spirit, so as our spirit knows it is spirit and therefore knows that healing works, why would it need our physical being to have faith for it to work?

Do you need any special tools to give spiritual healing?

No. You do not need anything other than a desire to heal. You do not need special clothes, magic sticks, wands, bells, incense, crystals or anything else. You are the tool! You do not even have to have the use of your limbs as you can project yourself to give healing, i.e. you can visualise yourself giving healing without leaving your bed, chair, home or wherever you happen to be. It is just a matter of practice. Some people find it easier to use tools as it helps them concentrate but this is a choice—you do not need to.

How long does it take to give someone healing?

How long is a piece of string! Healing takes as long as it takes or as long as the time you have available. Carole has given people healing in busy offices and the healing will stop just before the phones start ringing again. She has also given healing to a bus driver on a bus in a bus station while waiting to come home from work! As a rough guide it is normally about ten to fifteen minutes depending on circumstances. If time is not an issue or the person is elderly the healing may last much longer as it will come through more gently. If there is not much time it will come through in a more concentrated form. In either case the healing will continue for a period of time anyway, even when the healer has physically stopped channelling it.

If you are giving someone healing how do you know when to stop?

This is hard to explain because it is an instinctive feeling. You just know when it is time to stop.

What is crystal healing?

Healers sometimes use crystals when giving healing. A variety of crystals are placed on different parts of the body to enhance the healing. Each crystal has different properties and it is these properties that healers use. Crystals can also be used for protection. This is a very large subject and there is really not room to discuss it fully here. There are, however, many books on the subject and many teachers who will show you how to use crystals properly.

What is the difference between Reiki and spiritual healing?

Technically there is no difference. Reiki is a Japanese version of spiritual healing. In Reiki the healer lays their hands on the client whereas in spiritual healing the healer normally heals through the aura and therefore may not always touch the client. Many spiritual healers who also practise Reiki healing will often use both when they give healing. The only other difference is that spiritual healing is normally always given free.

Can you learn both at the same time?

When you first start learning Reiki you spend three weeks giving yourself Reiki every night. This is known as the cleansing period and the idea is to rid yourself of all the negative energy that you have accumulated and to prepare you to be able to give healing. If you have never meditated or had healing then you will need this period to begin the cleansing process. Self-cleansing is, of course, an ongoing process.

However, if you have been sitting regularly in circle, meditate regularly or have had healing regularly then the self-cleansing is really just a ritual as most of the really deep cleansing will have already happened. Even if you are new to healing then there is nothing to stop you learning both together. They will complement each other.

Why do healers always seem to be ill or have had turbulent lives?

There are several reasons for this. If you were never ill or had never had any problems you would not have any empathy with other people. You cannot understand someone else's problems unless you have some experience of that problem. The same goes for physical pain. You are much more likely to open up to or have faith in someone if you know they have experienced something similar to you. This is because you know that they do have some understanding of the issues involved and the emotions you are feeling. Furthermore, if you never have any problems you could become arrogant and feel superior to other people. Other people would not feel comfortable coming to you because they would see you as some kind of super being! Healers are the same as everybody else: they have the same problems, the same gifts and they make the same mistakes. After all, it's by making mistakes that we learn and by learning we evolve.

What is the aura?

Contrary to popular belief our soul or spirit is not inside our body but outside. Quite simply the aura is our spirit and the relationship between this and our physical body is vibratory. The aura is rather like the atmosphere that surrounds the planet. The body is enclosed and interpenetrated by the aura. This sets up a vibratory relationship between the body and the aura. Shaped like an egg the aura can stretch up to 18 inches around the body. One of the reasons we find it uncomfortable when people stand too close to us without our permission is because they are standing in our personal space.

Our aura should be a balanced mix of all the colours. Purple is considered to be a high spiritual colour. Indigo is another spiritual colour. Blue is considered to be the healing colour. Green is considered to be the colour of humanity and pink the colour of love. Yellow is the colour of creativity. Orange is the colour associated with confidence. Red and black are considered to be the earthly base colours that provide grounding and stability. Healers often use these colours when they are giving healing.

But our aura changes colour as we come into contact with the negative emotions and thoughts of others and of the environment in which we live. These changes in colour reflect the imbalance that this contact causes.

Thus our aura reflects our physical and mental health and changes colour as our physical and emotional health changes. The physical and emotional effects of this imbalance can lead eventually to physical and emotional problems.

Healers heal through the aura by holding their hands at a distance of about six to ten inches away from the person they are giving healing to. If you hold your hands out palms facing each other about six to ten inches apart and then gradually push them together you can feel the aura.

There are now cameras with special filters that can be used to photograph the aura.

What is colour therapy?

Colour is an integral part of our life. The sun's electromagnetic energy includes light. Our eyes reflect the wavelengths of this energy and interpret it into the various hues of the colour spectrum. The combination of the receptive ability of our eyes, and the gases, moisture and dust particles of the earth's atmosphere refract the light into colour. Each colour has its own individual characteristics and effects and imbalances in the colours cause physical and emotional problems. Colour healing was used in the temples of ancient Egypt, Greece, China, India and Tibet. Colour therapy is a holistic therapy that works on freeing the energy flow of the body by projecting colour back into our aura.

Why do some people feel worse after healing?

Very occasionally the healing is held within the aura to be released gradually. This may mean the person may feel worse to start with but will then feel much better.

What are chakras?

There is a misconception that chakras are psychic centres and have to be "opened" and "closed" to enable us to talk to sprit. As we have already discussed, talking to spirit involves raising our consciousness, always ensuring we use the white light for protection. Chakras are energy centres, they cannot be opened and closed but can be out of balance and can be energised. There are seven main chakras: each is a different colour and corresponds to a different area of the body and has positive and negative qualities. The following is a brief definition of the seven chakras:

The crown chakra is located at the crown or top of the head and the colour associated with it is purple. The areas of the body to which it corresponds are the cerebral cortex, the central nervous system, the pineal gland and the right eye. Amongst the positive qualities associated with the crown chakra are inspiration and idealism, unity with spirit, selflessness, divine wisdom and understanding. Its negative qualities are generally the opposite including lack of inspiration, depression, confusion and alienation.

Located in the centre of the forehead between the eyebrows is the brow chakra. Associated with the pituitary gland, left eye, nose and ears, its colour is indigo. Some of the positive qualities associated with the brow chakra are intuition and wisdom, clairvoyance, concentration and imagination and peace of mind. Its negative qualities include lack of concentration, headaches and tension, fear, cynicism, bad dreams and eye problems.

The throat chakra is in the throat and its colour is blue. Associated with the thyroid, parathyroid, hypothalamus, throat and mouth, its positive qualities are communication, creativity in speech, writing and the arts, peace, truth, knowledge and wisdom, honesty and reliability, gentleness and kindness. Amongst the negative qualities associated with it are communication and/or speech problems, lack of discernment and thyroid problems.

In the centre of the chest is the heart chakra and the colour associated with it is green. Associated with the heart, thymus gland, circulatory system, arms, hands and lungs, it has several positive qualities including unconditional love, forgiveness, compassion and understanding, balance, harmony and contentment. Repression and emotional instability, heart and circulation problems are just some of its negative qualities.

The solar plexus chakra is located below the chest, above the navel. It is connected with the liver, muscles, gallbladder, nervous system, pancreas, adrenals and the stomach and its colour is yellow. Its positive qualities include authority, energy, self-control, radiance, warmth, humour and laughter. Its negative qualities include too much emphasis on power and recognition, anger and fear, hate and digestive problems.

The navel chakra is positioned in the lower abdomen. It is associated with the colour orange, the ovaries, womb and bladder, testicles, prostate, genitals and spleen. Its positive qualities include emotions, giving and receiving, desire and pleasure, assimilation of new ideas, health and tolerance. Greed, sexual difficulties, jealousy, envy, possessiveness, uterine and bladder problems are some of its negative qualities.

The base chakra is located at the base of the spine (coccyx). Its colour is red/black and it is associated with the colon, kidneys, adrenals, spinal column, bones and legs. Its positive qualities often relate to physical matters of the world including success, security, grounding and stability, individuality, courage and patience. Selfishness, insecurity, violence, greed, anger, spinal tension and constipation are the negative qualities associated with the base chakra.

This is just a brief look at the chakras. If you wish to know more there are plenty of books around that will give you a more in-depth explanation including some of the books on yoga.

How do you give healing to your family?

Ask the member of the family to sit or lie down comfortably and close their eyes. Make sure they uncross their arms and legs—this is because crossed arms and legs become uncomfortable after a while and the idea is for the person to relax! Either stand or sit down behind them making sure you are comfortable too. Tell them that you will put your hands on their shoulders when you start and again when you finish and that it will probably last about five to fifteen minutes. The most effective healing comes through in the first five to fifteen minutes. Then ask them either: to visualise themselves somewhere they like being (the beach, countryside, etc) or to visualise a wall of their favourite colour in front of them and when they feel your hands on their shoulders they should walk into this wall and allow the colour to surround them.

First you protect yourself with the white light (see Chapter 7). You should always protect yourself with this white light before you do anything spiritual. Then ask in your head for only the highest and the best and then ask for your healing guides to come forward. Ask (pray) that the person you wish to give healing to is healed if it is meant to be. Use your own words and mean it. Visualise a white light around the person you are going to give healing to and then touch them lightly on the shoulders. Hold your hands, palms open, over the shoulders of the person and visualise a blue light coming out through the palms of your hands and covering the whole of the person. Concentrate on that image for as long as you feel comfortable. If the colour changes—let it. Healing will go to the place it is needed but if you feel the need to move your hands so they are over another part of the body then go ahead. You do not need to touch the person at all. You are healing through the aura.

You may find your hands get hot or tingle or shake. That's great—it means the energy is flowing through you. On the other hand you may feel nothing. That doesn't mean it isn't working. Stop when you feel it is time, thank your healing guides and allow the white light to go back to its original size. Then touch the person on the shoulders to let them know the healing is finished. Have some water handy so you can both have a drink. Healing always works; it just doesn't always work in the way we think it is going to! Often people ask for healing because they have a physical ache or pain. However, this physical ache may be caused by emotional problems and often the healing will concentrate on the emotional issues and when they are resolved the physical may follow suit.

Is there a scientific proof that healing works?

Japanese researchers set up cameras that recorded infra red and other frequencies and filmed a healer giving healing to a patient. The healer was giving healing from a distance of about 18 in–2 ft. The film showed the energy coming from the hands of the healer and showed that the knees of the patient were red—a sign of the heat that the patient could feel.

In the North Hawaii Community Hospital eleven healers were asked to give distant healing to someone they felt close to whilst they were in a scanner. This scanner uses pulses of

111

high intensity magnetic fields to build up a 3D picture of the body. Any changes in localised brain activity would show up as changes in the magnetic imaging of blood flow and this would be colour coded onto an outline of the brain.

The healers stayed in an electromagnetically-shielded control room whilst their friends were in another room in the scanner. They were then asked to send healing in two-minute bursts, with intervals in between, on command. The experiment for each healer lasted about 35 minutes and began with establishing the baseline blood flow values of the person in the scanner.

During the interval time for every healer the blood flow remained at the baseline level, but when the healers sent healing the blood flow increased to areas in the deep brain which is known as the limbic system. This is the part of the brain that deals with body awareness and the emotional sense of the self. It is here that the brain's own pain-relieving hormones are stored. Although science is still unable to explain healing in a scientific way it accepts that healing does work—it just can't be explained yet!

How can healing be used for the common good?

A recent documentary set out to try and prove that there was no scientific basis to healing. Unfortunately it did not use either of the two methods above and spent most of the programme concentrating on placebos. It finally concluded that healing only worked because the patients believed that it did. This is something that is obviously disputed by the above examples. However, if the so-called placebo effect made the patient better, then presumably they didn't need medicine in the first place? In this instance the patient could have been given expensive drugs, which may or may not have had side effects which they obviously didn't need. Instead they were "cured." This saved the NHS money which of course saves us money.

The money saved by giving healing to people instead of expensive drugs can be used to treat other illnesses and diseases. We have been given the gift of our brains so that we can discover cures for all manner of afflictions but there are many afflictions that are spiritual and can therefore be cured spiritually.

What is self-healing?

This is an interesting question and the answer is really in two parts. In the sense of contact healing, self-healing does not exist. This is because healers act as channels for the energy and healing that comes from spirit. They are not the healer so in this sense they would not be healing themselves!

If you have a pain or you feel that you need healing, just follow the guidelines for "healing friends and family" above but put your hands over or on the affected area and ask for healing. (Don't forget your protection!) There is no reason that you cannot ask for healing for yourself. It is no different from going to another healer and asking for healing.

However, there are many other ways that we can heal ourselves.

How can you heal yourself?

"Purity of the mind is not possible without purity of the body in which it functions, and by which it is affected."

Swami Vishnu—Devananda

We have looked at how we can change our world by including a spiritual aspect to our lives. We can now look at how our lifestyle in general can help to heal ourselves and our environment. No, it's not going to be a long lecture on the environment or tell you that you should live a life of abstinence! We all know how to improve the environment and living a life of abstinence would rather defeat the object! If you don't "live" how can you experience anything? This is more about the choices that we make.

Diet

There are thousands of books, magazines and websites devoted to telling us what we should and shouldn't eat and you don't need us to add to them! All we would like to say is that if you try to make sure your diet contains plenty of unprocessed foods, fresh fruit and vegetables and lots of whole grains you will go a long way to improving not only your health but also on cutting down the amount of carbon and waste we produce.

If you can shop locally this will also provide local employment so people will not have to travel so far to work; the food will be fresher because it will not have travelled so far or been stored for so long, and it is likely to have less packaging. You may find you can walk to do the shopping which reduces carbon emissions and gives you some exercise! We appreciate that this is not always possible and there are many reasons people do not do this. You don't need suddenly to change all your shopping habits. But try just changing how you buy a portion of your shopping—maybe the vegetables or the bread.

If we all start to do this it introduces more competition into the market place which is good for us (so politicians tell us!) and it will start to have an impact on other areas of our lives. If we are all healthier we will save the NHS millions. If we are healthier we will enjoy ourselves more because we will have more energy and so on. If we are able to work locally it means we have more time to spend with our families which will strengthen the bonds we have with our partners and children. No—it is not likely to make much difference if just one or two people do it (except to them!) but what if one or two million do it?

We have tried to give you a brief overview of how the practical aspects of healing can benefit us politically and socially.

The next chapter lays out the seven principles on which our spiritual framework is based.

Chapter 11

The Principles

"Peace comes within the souls of men when they realise their relationship, their Oneness, with the universe and all its powers; and when they realise that at the centre of the universe dwells Great Spirit, and that this centre is really everywhere. It is within each of us."
                                        Black Eye, Native American Visionary

"So, let us not be blind to our differences - but let us also direct attention to our common interests and to the means by which those differences can be resolved."
                                        John F. Kennedy

ALL frameworks or theories have to be based on something and our spiritual framework draws on the common ground between science, politics, religion and spiritualism. This common ground which we have identified as our morality is in fact our spirituality and can best be articulated as follows:

1. We are one

Religion and spiritualism tells us we are all one. Science tells us that we all originate from the same gene pool, and are in fact related to each other, however distantly.

Politically, we are told, the good of one is the good of all (the common good). We need to have a common good or we would not have a society. This does not mean that our perception of the common good is the same. Nor does it mean that we are all the same and that our interests are all the same. But we do have to live together and our society is the form that we have chosen to do this.

Religions and spiritualism tell us that we are all one spirit. We are all on our separate pathways but they are all linked. We do not exist in isolation and every decision we make affects someone else. Therefore, if we are all one, what we do to others we do to ourselves. Conversely what we do to ourselves we do to others. If we do not love ourselves we cannot love anybody else. We are aiming to love unconditionally but this must also be applied to ourselves. We need to have respect to love but we cannot respect each other if we have no self-respect. We are here to learn and we are here to help our children learn. We need to teach our children that when you are learning you make mistakes. If we were perfect we would not need to be here! Accept yourself and aim to be the best you can be and help others to be the best they can be.

2. We are one with the planet and all beings that co-exist here

Without our planet we would not be here. On a scientific level our actions and lifestyles are causing global warming and the extinction of many species. Politically, the decisions we make, the leaders we elect, the choices we make are causing these environmental problems. But we have also chosen the planet to be like it is by our thoughts, words and actions. Remember nothing happens here that is not controlled by us or that we are not responsible for. If we learn to control our thoughts, words and actions we will begin to make a different type of world, a different type of society.

We need to evolve quicker while we are here or we will continue to have mass "natural" disasters. Choosing to live our lives spiritually will help us to do this. If we live according to these principles we will all evolve quicker and decelerate the destruction of our planet and consequently fewer people will die.

The planet is getting old. We need to treat it better than we treat our older people. As people become older they are more vulnerable so they need more care. The same can be said of our planet. When people get older they have accumulated a certain amount of wisdom. We need to utilise this wisdom in our society. In the same way we need to look at some of the methods and practices that ancient civilisations had of caring for and living as one with their environment. Young and modern is not necessarily the best.

3. We choose to live our lives with love, peace, compassion, tolerance, humanity, humility, understanding and kindness— in other words we choose to live spiritually

All of these are unconditional, non-judgmental and given in generosity of spirit and in the service of others. In other words we give all these to others without expecting anything in return. However, this will only work if everyone is prepared to do the same. This is only likely to happen when we have all changed our perceptions of why we are here and consequently we have all evolved further.

We do not judge each other or ourselves because we are not judged. We can assess our lives and those of others and we can offer advice and help and constantly aim to improve and be the best that we can be and help others to do the same. This does not mean we have to buy every product that comes out in pursuit of looking eternally young. It means finding the balance between accepting that we are getting older and making the effort to look as good as we reasonably can. It means accepting that we are not all meant to look the same or have the same body shape. It doesn't mean ruthlessly stepping on everybody in an attempt to have more money, more wealth, more status. It means accepting that although we are one, we are, paradoxically, all different and we all have different paths to tread. It means not squandering our talents but using them for the benefit of all. It means living our lives to the full and accepting that we are not perfect and nor is anyone else.

When we die we will go Home and evaluate our lives. The mistakes we have made are part of our learning process, but the more we evolve the fewer mistakes we will make and the fewer times we will have to come back. It's rather like having a list and ticking off those lessons that you have completed. As we all evolve to that stage the world will become a place that we will be happy to come back to because it will be a place of light and love.

117

If we try at all times to give love, whether in words, by a smile, in acts of kindness or by a simple hug or hand holding, then everybody wins. Whether you are a scientist or already have a religious belief or you are a total agnostic you cannot deny the logic of this last sentence. When we understand this basic message of unconditional love and healing, then the answer to the question "why are we here?" becomes clear. We are here to learn—to advance—to evolve spiritually. We do this by helping one another to learn—advance—and evolve spiritually. What we give to others we receive back one hundredfold. If we all live our lives with this in mind—or in soul—think how much more developed, advanced and evolved our world would be.

4. We believe our spirit is eternal and our purpose here is to evolve

As physical beings we, like the planet, are constantly evolving. Although this has historically been a slow process our activities and the way we live our lives is causing that process to speed up. To ensure our planet survives we must also speed up our evolution. We do this by being the best we can be. Not at the expense of others but in service of others. By being the best we can be, by constantly striving to go that extra mile we will be happy. If you are bored with your job find another one. If you're bored you won't be doing your job properly anyway. Let somebody new come in with enthusiasm and new ideas. Don't dismiss new ideas without careful thought. There may be good reasons to carry on doing things in a certain way. But are they good reasons? Are they in the best interests of everybody or only a few?

We need to evolve politically as well. Our current systems of government and our monetary systems do not seem to be working. Capitalism is based on a system that needs constant expansion and consumption but for both the planet and capitalism to survive there needs to be a re-evaluation of this. Is it possible to find a system that works on sustainable consumption? Or is it necessary to keep consuming more and more? Is it time to look for a system that provides sufficient for all instead?

5. We choose to use our gifts for the benefit of all

We all have gifts and they can all be used in either a positive way or a negative way. They have not been distributed arbitrarily; we have chosen them. It is therefore our choice how we use them. But this freedom of choice carries responsibility. There are always those who will abuse that freedom of choice. We can see that in the way positive ideas and actions are often thwarted and misused. The original good intention becomes lost or subsumed beneath the more negative use that is more widely publicised.

Many groups that are set up for all sorts of good reasons find that they achieve a certain amount and then it all falls apart. Bickering, in-fighting, egos and gossip put an end to all the good ideas and plans. But it doesn't have to be like that. We are all human and we all have egos. Our egos are another gift and how we use them is our choice.

Remember why you started the group in the first place and ask yourself whether it is your spirit or your ego that is making the decisions. This doesn't mean that you should tolerate people walking all over you (remember the discussion about tolerance in Chapter 3), just that you should always re-examine your own motives first before you do or say anything. Our world needs balance and so do we. Finding the line between arrogance and confidence (ego and spirit), is just one of the lessons we are here to learn.

We can also see the misuse of our gifts in science when a discovery that is for the benefit of human kind is hijacked and used for other purposes. Being able to detect the sex of a foetus was intended to be used to screen out inherited diseases but is now being used by people who are under pressure to have a child of a particular sex. This will eventually affect the balance of the gender ratio in the world. Historically, it does not herald a particularly peaceful world when the ratio of boys to girls is out of balance.

This abuse of positive gifts can also be seen in spiritualism. Although there are excellent mediums and healers who genuinely wish to use their gifts to help promote love, peace and harmony, there are also those whose motives are less clear. The aim of genuine mediums and healers is to make themselves redundant! If we do our job properly everybody will know how to heal and everyone will know how to talk to spirit.

6. We choose to share

We choose to share everything—resources, money, knowledge, etc. Although resources are finite there are enough for everyone to have sufficient. Technological advances mean that in the future the resources we have can be used in a sustainable way.
There is also more than enough money to ensure that everybody has enough to eat, clean water to drink, and somewhere decent to live. We are not saying that everybody should be equal just that everybody should have sufficient for their needs. The definition of sufficiency is something to discuss at a later date. The point of these principles is to lay down the framework. As we said at the beginning—the rest is mere details!

It is also important that we all share knowledge. We all live here so we are all entitled to know what is happening. But the knowledge that we share needs to be unbiased and independent. This may prove to be one of the greatest challenges we face. It is difficult to provide unbiased knowledge but not impossible. At present there is a tendency for the world's information to be provided by a few. This means that our view of the world is the view that the few wish us to have. By learning how to meditate and listen to spirit we will ensure that we all have access to the information we need to make informed decisions. If the messages we are given are inclusive of all we will know that we are interpreting them in the right way. This means totally inclusive of all. If the interpretation is in any way exclusive then it has been interpreted in the wrong way.

7. We choose to make our world a better place to live

It is our world, our planet. We are the politicians, we are the scientists, we are the religious leaders, we are the consumers. We are the media. We are the people. There is no-one else. It is our responsibility to ensure that the world is a better place for our children and grandchildren and for future generations to come. It is our choice to make our world a better place to live now.

Our world thrives on light and the warmth of the sun. Virtually all living things grow and develop either directly or indirectly in the light and warmth of the sun including us. Our spiritual pathway also depends on the use of light. The white light of the Creator/God/Allah/The Great Mind provides our protection and illuminates our way. However,

"God has so created His sons and His daughters
that they themselves must release the light before it
can act in them and in their outer lives."

(Morning Light—White Eagle 1994)

Releasing our own light is easy; we just have to choose to do to it. (See Chapter 6, Meditation)

By becoming en-light-eners, we can not only bring light to our own lives, but also to the lives of all those we meet. By becoming en-lighten-ers we can also help lighten the load of our fellow travellers. If we all become enlighteners our world will change beyond recognition.

Chapter 12

Spiritual Centres

"Sometimes our light goes out but is blown into flame by another human being. Each of us owes deepest thanks to those who have rekindled this light."

Albert Schweitzer

IT may not be necessary or even an objective for most people to want to set up their own spiritual centre but if you would like to these are some suggestions either for now or for future reference.

First and foremost you are your own spiritual centre. You do not need anyone else with you to meditate or to send absent healing. However, it is nice and the vibrations are often stronger, if you meditate with other people and part of our role in this life is to help others. One of the main points of this book is to explain that we are all entitled to know why we are here. If we all know that we will act differently and our world will change accordingly. By passing on this philosophy and the ideas contained within this book we hope that other people will be helped and in turn this will help us as we all have to live here.

Spiritually we may all be at different levels and all have different talents and abilities and different tasks to carry out. But this does not mean that one spirit is more important than any other spirit. Being a medium or a healer does not make one person more important than anyone else. We are all special and we can all be mediums or healers if we choose to do so.

Premises

If you decide that you would like to set up your own centre the first thing to think about is where you are going to have it. Do you want to have a few friends round to your house once a week or once a fortnight or do you want to find a larger place that is open to the public?

If you just want to have a few friends round to your house you can still follow the suggestions further on for mediums, format, healing, etc. You may even find that you start by using your home and then find that it is so popular you need to hire somewhere.

If you decide that you would like to find a building that you can invite the public to, you need to think about how many people are likely to attend. There is no point hiring a building the size of the Albert Hall if you are only realistically likely to have a regular attendance of a couple of dozen!

When you have found a likely building you need to find out how much it is to hire and whether you can have it on a regular basis.

Frequency

The next issue to decide is how often you wish to meet. This also needs to be realistic. But it is also important to try and meet on the same day and time, whether it is weekly, fortnightly or monthly.

Advertising

Presumably you will already know what sort of demand there is before you look at hiring premises. But it is always good to have new people come and they won't be able to unless they know you are there. Unless you have lots of money you will want to find the cheapest way of advertising. This can include posters, cards in shop windows, websites of other centres and notice boards in community centres and offices. You can also produce your own leaflets explaining who you are and the kinds of things your centre offers.

As one of our roles in life is to help other people it would be good to share any profits that you make with a local charity. This in turn will help with advertising, help the local charity and spread the word at the same time. Everybody benefits. As your centre expands you can consider setting up your own website with links to other websites and so on.

Costs

The idea of the spiritual centre is not to make vast sums of money. It is to help people by explaining how they can help themselves. This means keeping charges to a minimum. Some of the best centres we have been to charge an entrance fee of about £3-£5 (at time of writing). For this you have an evening of clairvoyance, a question and answer session, free healing, and free tea, coffee and biscuits. Our services at West Mersea and Kelvedon also include a workshop and free copies of spiritual magazines. Most centres also have raffles which consist of two or three small prizes as this is a good way of raising a little bit of extra money and often the money from these raffles goes to local charities.

Mediums

Genuine mediums will be happy to come to your centre providing you can cover their travelling expenses. Some will take less if they know you are just starting out. If you are setting up a centre and would like to contact us we will try and help you find some mediums to start you off.

Healing

If you are going to offer healing to members of the public you will need either to train as a healer or find some healers that have certificates with one of the reputable organisations and are therefore insured. Although this may seem a little extreme it is for your own protection. If you allow someone who is not a certificated healer to give healing and there is a problem you will be responsible. Once you are up and running you will find healing organisations that are training healers will be happy to bring their trainees along. The healing they will give will be as good as that of a certificated healer but they need to practise to cover the requisite number of hours and to fulfil their full potential. They will always be accompanied by their trainer or another certificated healer. If you have trained to be a healer you may wish to teach healing yourself as you will meet plenty of people through the centre who wish to become healers. Healing can either be before the service, during it or afterwards and should be available to all including children and animals. (Remember that children should always have their parents and guardians present and animal owners must have consulted their vet if the animal is sick and must give their permission).

Workshops

A good way of helping to stimulate interest is to either run a workshop after your service or ask the visiting medium if they would like to run a workshop. If this is included in the entrance price it will be affordable for all and help to make people feel really welcome and a part of the centre. It will also help them to develop their own abilities.

Children

Most centres are happy for you to bring your children with you as long as they are well behaved. Alternatively you can have another room for the children to play in if they are supervised by their own parents or approved adult. They are the future so it is important that they are included. But you should always remember that children are more vulnerable so you should always ensure that you use your white light to strengthen the protection around your centre.

Format

This is really up to you but we would ask that you always start with an opening prayer to thank the guides and helpers who are going to be there and to ask for protection for all those present. You can follow this by teaching your gathering to use the white light. Explain why you are doing this and explain that if they wish to communicate with spirit at any time they should always do this first. Explain how it is their protection and that it will also ensure that spirit is able to come through more clearly because the vibrations are higher. This helps to get everybody involved and turns your audience into participants. It will also ensure your building has the protection you need and raise the vibrations to the highest level. Collectively your light will be really strong and it will protect you all from the odd visitor whose light may not be as white as it should be.

This should always be followed by a healing minute because, as we explained earlier, the healing vibration is the highest vibration. The spokesperson will ask those present to begin by sending healing to the planet and every living being on the planet and then the places in the world where it is particularly needed, including mention of any specific events that are relevant at the time. This is followed by sending healing to all those on sick beds, in hospices and healing books and then there is a minute's silence while those present send healing to their own friends and loved ones. If you wish you can explain that sending healing can either be a prayer in their own words or they can visualise the planet and their loved ones and visualise a blue healing light round the planet and their loved ones whilst asking for healing. After this the format is pretty much up to you. The following are just suggestions:

It is nice to follow this with some music that everyone can sing along to. It's amazing how singing can raise the vibrations and the more upbeat the music the higher the |vibration. We would suggest a mixture of modern and older songs and/or hymns that everyone knows but you can tailor this to suit the average age or background of those present. If your gathering consists of teenagers and young adults they may not be too enthralled if you start playing hymns and conversely an older gathering may not be impressed if you play the latest chart hits!

The visiting medium can then give an address. As we explained in Chapter 8 an address is spiritual philosophy given by the medium in communication with spirit.

One way of getting those present involved is to ask them to bring a reading or poem or something they would like to share with everybody else. They can either read this out at a time to be agreed with you or someone else can read it out for them.

You can include as many songs and readings as you like and the people who are there want to have. Nothing is set in stone and you can change it as often as you feel is necessary.

At this point most services have the clairvoyant period. This is the time when the medium acts as a channel between loved ones and those on the earth plane. It usually lasts between 30 minutes and an hour and a half depending on the type of service. For instance, if there is a workshop afterwards the clairvoyance will be shorter.

Once the clairvoyant period is over you can have a question and answer session and when you are finished have a closing prayer in which you thank spirit for allowing you to meet and to thank your guides, helpers and loved ones for being there. Finish with a request that any remaining healing energy is sent to wherever it is needed and that those present are protected in the weeks to come and are able to help those they come in contact with.

The most important part of your centre is the atmosphere. It should be welcoming and inclusive. That is why the tea break is such an important time. There are many people who may welcome the chance to make new friends with people who are like minded and this is the ideal opportunity. The tea break allows people to meet each other and to discuss any problems that they have and if there is a workshop after the tea break more people will be encouraged to stay.

We hope these guidelines are helpful but they are only guidelines. It is your spiritual centre and you will have your own ideas of how it should run. If we can help in any way please contact us.

In the meantime here are some contact details of useful organisations:

You can contact us on 01621 869567
E-mail saahera@tiscali.co.uk
or visit our website at
www.saahera-centre.org

We also run regular services on Mersea Island on the second Tuesday of every month and in Kelvedon on the 4th Tuesday of every month. For more details including the names of visiting mediums please see the website.

For an example of a very welcoming centre visit The Guiding Light in Hayes, Middlesex. For further information contact 0208 797 7733 or visit their website on
        http://freespace.virgin.net/russel.st/index.htm
        At present they meet every Friday at 7pm.

Other useful contacts:

        United Spiritualists
        www.unitedspiritualists.org.uk

        UK Healers
        www.ukhealers.info

        Essex Spirit Guide
        http://www.EssexSpiritGuide.co.uk

        The Psychic News/The Psychic Press
        http://www.psychicnewsbookshop.co.uk

Chapter 13

The End of the Beginning

"Man must evolve for all human conflict a method which rejects revenge, aggression and retaliation. The foundation of such a method is love."

Martin Luther King Jr.

"Our scientific power has outrun our spiritual power. We have guided missiles and misguided men."

Martin Luther King Jr., Strength to Love, 1963

"You must be the change you want to see in the world."

Mahatma Gandhi

WE will begin the final chapter by tying up all the seemingly diverse threads of our introduction to life that are covered in the previous chapters.

We started by looking at how religions and spiritualism are culturally and spatially specific. This just means that they were specific to the culture and time in which they were written. They are all interpretations of the same message but written in the language and understanding of the authors of the time. We argued that it is now time to reinterpret this message and bring it up to date so that it is specific to the cultures and times in which we are all living now. They were also written in a time when religions gave people their collective identity. We also looked at how collective identities can lead to the exclusion or vilification of others. We have argued that as citizens of one world, it is time to move away from narrow forms of collective identity and to find an identity that accurately reflects this new collective understanding.

This is not without precedent. In the 4th century the Emperor Constantine did exactly that. In order to bring peace to the Roman Empire, which was in danger of disintegrating because of the diverse beliefs and cultures of the many groups within its borders, he amalgamated all the diverse religious beliefs of these groups into what we now know as Christianity. He did it by force—we are arguing that it is now time to do this by choice. It is now time to introduce a new interpretation of the message which draws together all the spiritual elements we all have in common. We all work on love and light and in the name of the common good of humanity so let's start there. Any other differences of interpretation can be negotiated into a spiritual framework that we can all subscribe to.

We looked at how politics could use this spiritual framework to provide one shared moral identity that could cement the diverse cultural and social groups within society together for the common good.

We also discussed how science could also be part of this framework. Historically, science and religion have been seen as diametrically opposed. Although this gap has narrowed over the years there is still a perception that you cannot believe in both science and religion. We have argued that this is actually a false perception. Modern science frequently incorporates ethical considerations as a matter of course. The shared cultural values of society already restrict what scientists can and cannot do. The majority of scientists already work for the benefit of humankind so they already share the same common ground as proponents of both religion and spiritualism.

We then proceeded to begin to answer the most fundamental questions: who we are, where do we come from and why we are here? We explained how we choose our lives so that we can experience the emotions, feelings and sensations that we cannot experience as spirit. We explained about our gifts and how we can use all our gifts, even the seemingly negative ones, in positive ways for the good of all. By understanding that we are all spirit we can see how we are all one. How the suffering of one is the suffering of all, spiritually, politically and scientifically. By understanding that this is but one life we can see how important it is to change the world in which we live for the better. For if we don't, when we come back again it may be even worse. This is one way we can use our gift of selfishness for the good of all. We also looked at the power of our thoughts and emotions and how they impact on the world and how the world in turn impacts on our thoughts and emotions.

We continued by trying to see how our politicians could help us to feel more involved in the decisions that affect us. Like religion, spiritualism and science, politicians also claim to work for the good of the people who represent them. Unfortunately, as less than half the country bother to vote, most of us are not really represented. This leaves the door open to extremists. By changing the way we choose our representatives we may start to feel more involved and if we feel more involved we can begin to make a difference.

Chapter 6 explained what meditation was and how it can be used to help us find our own answers to these questions. We showed how science in the form of our health services accepts the benefits of meditation and is now actively encouraging us to practise meditation on a regular basis. We explained the importance of protection and how it is imperative that we learn to use our white light and that we use it before we communicate with spirit. We then talked you through meditations and explained how to get the best from these and looked at ways in which both science and politics are already benefiting from the practical aspects of our spiritual framework.

Chapter 7 looked in detail at mediumship. It examined the different types of mediumship and the different ways mediums work. It explained how you can develop your abilities and the different types of development groups available. It finished with a look at how the advances in technology are enabling science to prove the existence of spirit and how politics (through the police and armed forces) are already using mediumship.

Chapter 8 looked at the most frequently asked questions to do with mediums and readings. It also explained that visiting a medium or attending a clairvoyant sitting is an interactive event. By participating you will raise the vibrations of the event and enable the medium to channel the messages easier. The quality of the messages will be much higher and you will enjoy yourself much more if you take part and we explained how you could do this.

Chapter 9 began by looking at the dangers posed by Ouija boards and other means of communicating with spirit without using protection and continued by answering questions about miscarriage, organ donation, what happens to those who commit suicide and whether karma exists.

Chapter 10 explored the many types of spiritual healing that we can all do including absent healing. It explained how you can send healing and how you can give "contact" healing to your friends and family. The chapter continued by looking at some of the scientific experiments that have taken place in different parts of the world which showed that healing does work and is effective. This led to a discussion of the political benefits that healing on a wider scale could bring including how changes to our lifestyles will achieve self-healing.

In Chapter 11 we laid out the seven principles that form the basis of this spiritual framework and discussed them in detail. We ended by pointing out that we are the only ones who can change our world. As this is a spiritual handbook we thought it would be useful to give you some ideas and suggestions as to how to run your own spiritual centre, so Chapter 12 explained some possible ways you could do this and gave some contact details of useful organisations.

Although this book is concerned with helping to shape a better future it is also concerned with shaping a better today. We are all so busy we do not have time to live in the present. It has been said many times but it is worth repeating. The present is a gift. That is why it is called the present.

Our planet is wonderful. We do not have to look far to find beauty in both the planet and the people. We can see it in the flowers, in the beautiful countryside, in the oceans and continents. We can see it in the first snow of winter and the first sign of spring, in the sweet songs of birds and the music of the jungles and the rainforests. We can see beauty in the people who spend their lives quietly trying to help others. We can see it in our smiles and in our children's laughter. But we believe that there is a danger that this beauty will be lost to us and to future generations. Our present and our future are closely linked both physically and spiritually. By changing our present we can ensure our future is better.

You've read the book and by now you must have had some thoughts about what you have read. It is your world too. What do you think? Do you wake up every day thinking how wonderful the world is or do you look round in despair?

All we are asking is that you take some time to think of how you would like your world to be. See it, visualise it and say you choose for it to be that way – a world of love, peace, harmony and light. A world in which everyone has sufficient, everyone has equal access to resources, justice and the political system and everyone is free.

Isn't that better than what we have now?

A Final Message From Spirit

It all comes down to love. Without love there is nothing. Only love can cure the ills of the world and only love can cure the ills of your personal lives. Only love can bring peace because to be at peace you have to love and to love you have to be at peace.

Your world is beautiful; it is only your activities that render it ugly. Your thoughts words and actions have to change, only then will you begin to see the beauty around you. You, all of you, are ambassadors of light. If you were not you would not be reading this. As ambassadors of light it is for you to take this message far and wide.

The message is and always has been love, for it is only love that can change the world.

"In life, what sometimes appears to be the end is really a new beginning."

The End ?

Spirit Writings

THIS is a collection of writings received from spirit during various meditation and development groups from 2003–2007. We hope you enjoy reading them. Some were in response to questions that we were intending to include in this book but weren't sure of the answers. Others were questions that were asked that actually gave us the original idea for the book. The originals are in a variety of different handwriting, including a Greek-type script. However, they were actually physically written by one person.

Thursday May 8, 2003

Freedom is a choice like any other. You can be free if you wish. Spirit will guide you to freedom. You can leave behind the cares of the world if you see things differently. Your perceptions of life are all. They colour your experiences. See things spiritually and you are free. Freedom is yours—you just have to ask.

Life is not as it seems. This is your playground. All you have to do is evolve. Everything you experience is your choice. You choose this. Your instincts will guide you. We are your instincts. This is your soul speaking.

Upon this rock I will build my church. This church will be eternal because you are eternal and I am with you all to guide you. You just have to listen.

You are all the rocks, the foundations of the new world you will create. It's time you and the world evolved before you all have to move yet again.

I have given you a beautiful playground, yet like the children you are, you have spoilt it. You must grow up. This message is for you to pass on. That is why you will found the church. My church. Purple flowers will adorn my church—blue will colour them. Time is of the essence. The time is now.

You are my voice and you will share my knowledge. You do not have to learn, you have to remember. This is your freedom.

Monday May 12, 2003

The light shines for you all. The light will guide you. Love and light that is the direction you will lead my people. No longer will they toil and suffer, the light will set them free. My gifts to you all are wisdom, understanding, communication, compassion and love. Use these gifts to bring my people to the light. Suffer not for you will be saved from the toil of the day by following spirit. This is the message you must pass on. Spirit is there for all of you—not just a few. You are all chosen—you are each unique and at the same time you are all the same.

Listen to the word of spirit, my children. Pass them on. For my world to change you must all change. Time is running out. Help each other to understand. Let the light of freedom shine in your hearts. Let every fibre of your earthly being shine the light of spirit. Lead by example. It is the only way forward.

Welcome all seekers of the truth. They are the rocks and foundations. Like the pebbles thrown into a pond the ripples will extend outwards to reach every corner of the earth. Every thought, every word, every action will reflect my love. This example is what people will see and this example is what they will follow.

You are the light. Your thoughts words and actions should reflect this. It is time and the time is now.

Thursday May 22, 2003

What matters your religion? These are man made. Spirit has no religion yet is all religions. Just as spirit is both male and female so is spirit both religion and non-religion. This is a paradox I think. It is difficult for you to understand I know but it is important you take this message to the world because too often your people use religion as an excuse to kill each other. This must stop.

135

You must stop fighting over resources too. There is plenty to go round if you could only learn to share.

Love is about sharing. Sharing your goals, your future, your resources. This is why your world must learn to LOVE.
Now do you understand? LOVE is all.

Thursday May 22, 2003

Peace can be yours. Peace is always yours. You only have to ask. I am here to grant you that peace. First you have to listen to spirit. I will guide you. You have to listen carefully.

What I tell you can sometimes be misconstrued or misinterpreted. You know how easy it is to take the words of spirit and make them read what you wish. This is not our intention. We wish you to interpret our words for us so there is no misinterpretation.

Love is the most important gift we have to give you and you have to give each other. This is the first and most important lesson you have to pass on.

Love each other as you love yourself. For you cannot love each other if you do not love yourself. You are all one. We are all one. We are one with you. Therefore if you love yourself you will love others and if you love others you will love yourself.
So LOVE is the first lesson for you to pass on. This is the first step to PEACE.

We wish you to listen to us. LOVE is the first step towards PEACE. Peace is what your world desperately needs. And it can only be achieved through LOVE!

The second part of the tonight's message is strength. Strength and confidence to pass on our messages. Not everyone you pass these words to will be with you. Many will ridicule or try to malign you but these words will stand alone. They cannot be challenged because they are the truth. Time will prove this so you do not need to worry. We are always with you. You are our messengers.

Wednesday June 11, 2003

Love is always with you. Time will come when love is always with the world. The world will begin to appreciate the benefits of love.

Why fight when you can live in peace and harmony. Peace, harmony, these are all you need for a beneficial life.

Enjoy your lives. You are here to experience certain things. But they are not real because you are not your bodies—you are your soul.

Love is everything. This is the message you must pass on. Only when you understand what love is will you stop experiencing pain. This is the message for you to explain. If you are your soul you cannot really experience pain. Pain like happiness is in your mind. When you understand this you will be at the start of your journey. This is a first step. Time will help you to explain this. Time has no real meaning for your soul. If your current experiences seem bad they will not last. You have to feel the "bad" to appreciate the "good." As time has no meaning in real terms pain will soon pass.

This is very difficult for you to understand because you can only think in your human terms. But you are eternal. This life is but a blink of an eye in your real life. Your real life is your soul. This is the real you. The real you will go on in eternity and your experiences now will soon fade into insignificance. Evolve children, evolve.

Let me take you on a journey. A journey into the future. A life without pain, a life of love and only love.

Thursday July 24, 2003

> Ambassadors of light
> This is your call
> My word you will spread
> For all to hear

Do not fear the future
For the future you will shape
In my name forever more

Like the life you live
So will I share
My angel of light
With you for time immemorial

Spend no more time
Doubting or fearing
For I am your life
And love eternally

Inspired by love
These words will flow
For I am the guide
You have always known.

June/July 2003

Life's answers are there for those who wish to know. You only have to ask and your questions will be answered. Wars are not necessary. Wars are the sign of an immature world. It is time for you to go past this. Time to go beyond this base level. You are all able to heal. This is what you must pass on.

Go forth into the world and heal the people.

Saahera

Energy comes from the source. I am the source. You will use the energy to heal the people. So much pain—so much suffering. It does not have to be like this. You have the power within you to stop this. Why do you carry on suffering when you do not need to? This is not your reality. It is no more than one of your soap operas. Your reality is your soul. Many times do I tell you this. It is perhaps too difficult for you to grasp. Relax and believe. Nothing can hurt you for you are not here. Let your imagination guide you. Dream of all you wish for and it will become your reality. This is your choice. Chose happiness, chose love, chose to be at peace. This is your gift and one for you to pass on so all may be free.

Everything is balance. Your life should have balance. When you have found your balance you will be well on the way to understanding your purpose and you will begin to achieve the goals and targets that you are aiming for. You are finally on the right road. You know the answers just persevere a little longer and you will soon be where you want to be.

Together you will move mountains and you will change things. Not long now. It is slowly coming together. Time is irrelevant remember so don't be too impatient. This is your gift from me.

Thursday September 18, 2003

Saahera bids you all welcome. I have missed you all my friends. Opportunities are now limitless.

I wish to introduce myself to you. I am the angel of light and I am here to protect you. As you progress you will pick up more and more. You must therefore learn to protect yourself more. Your abilities are now increasing. Therefore your protection levels must also increase. I have given you the waterfall and mirrors. The cloak of invisibility is also helpful. The water of life is no longer pure. But life is not pure. It cannot be because only your spirit is pure. Your earthly body experiences all the emotions your spirit cannot. That is why you are here. To experience these emotions.

Do not despair when it seems there is no end to suffering. Suffering is really a product of the mind. Your spirit cannot suffer so you cannot really suffer or be hurt. It is just your mind's perception. Step back from your pain and remember who you really are. You are spirit.

Ask of life no more than what you can experience. Change your perception of the world and you will be happy. Remember all emotions are produced by your mind.

My blessings on you all. Take my message far and wide and remember:

139

Blue is the colour of my love
Purple is the colour of divine love
You are me and love is forever yours.
Golden is my protection and my cloak of love
Is always there
The most important message of all is love
Love heals
Love is kind
Love is compassion
Love is tolerance
Love is acceptance
Surrender to the divine
For the divine is love

Thursday September 25, 2003

It is for you to understand the problems of your life. I can answer only if you listen to the answers. Your mind is the root of all your emotions. But your spirit is stronger. Learn to control your mind by using the gifts I have given you. Your instincts are your guides. They will answer your questions. By controlling your mind you will have peace. I know this is difficult for you to grasp but as you persevere all will become clear.

Enter here and I will show you your future. Come with me and I will guide you.

I am the light that shines within, your protection. Enter the halls of wisdom with me. I have so much to show you. Life is unfolding for you. Relax and enjoy.

Wisdom is yours if you ask. But like everything you ask for there is a reciprocal action. We work in partnership with you. To receive wisdom you must learn to sieve through the lies. To seek truth you must have discernment. To have discernment you have to learn to trust your instincts. Your instincts will tell you whether you are being lied to. Listen to your instincts. They are your soul.

Everything in life is a balance. Too much detachment and you are not experiencing life. Too little detachment and you will be in pain. Find balance. Seek balance and harmony through meditation and healing. This you can do because these gifts I have given you.

Smile. Life can only improve as you learn to use your gifts. The gifts I am helping you develop. Your trials and problems are there to help you increase in awareness. Negativity can be overcome. You can protect yourself. Just remember who you really are. You are spirit. You are love. You are me and I am you.

Thursday May 25, 2006

We have always been with you. But you were not always able to see us. Your science and your religion penalised those who thought they saw or could see spirit. Religion and science are very close. Both like to control and therefore they both see spirituality as a threat. This may seem a little strange but religion is based on their version of spirituality. True spirituality/spiritualism as you call it is individual contact with spirit. You do not need someone else doing it for you. Each new generation needs more proof because of religion and science, so each generation is given the means to have a new way of proving our existence—hence the ability of each generation to develop new technology.

We like to visit when sometimes your cameras capture our images, sometimes not. We wish for images to be captured so you have the proof you need but we also have to learn and practise so our vibration can be captured in a form you can recognise.

One of the ways I wish you to spread my word is by the internet. Your pictures and words will be available to the world and provide the proof they need.

July 2006

The physical body and all its components all bear imprints from the spiritual essence of the person. Thus when we donate organs a vibration from our spirit will go with it. Yes, this does include the blood because the blood is touched by the vibration of spirit the same as any other organ. We are mind, body and spirit, remember. The three are intertwined and interconnected. The

141

imprint of spirit is on all. But this does not mean the personality of the person is also passed on. Only the part of the personality that is the spiritual essence of the person. It is possible that the person who has died and passed on their organs will come back to be the guide and helper. Sometimes this is written in the tapestry but it is not always the case and it does not have to be the case. The imprint of spirit on the organs and tissues is like a genetic fingerprint in that each is unique to that person. Yes, organ donation is right. If you have no need of something why would you want to keep it, bury it or burn it? You cannot take it with you! You leave other things, why not your body—your physical shell.

Thursday August 17, 2006

Let the world be your inspiration. Ideas and inspiration come from the source. The world is the source of many ideas and inspirations but they also come from your spiritual self. Take the idea of a smile. A smile can mean so many things to so many people. It is a sign of giving, a sign of receiving; a sign of love, a sign of peace. All these things are apparent in a smile. So why do you not all smile more often? There is so much beauty in a smile and so much pain in a frown. Think how your smile affects others. A smile can save a life, a smile can make a day. So much, so many things in something so simple. A smile is a gift the same as love is a gift. As with all gifts they should be used wisely. For a smile can also wound if used wrongly. Your humour is for you to laugh at yourselves, at your problems, at your mistakes. It is not for you to laugh at each other unless you are laughing with them. Never laugh at—only with and you will be using your gift of laughter to make the world a better place. Remember—a smile costs nothing and gives everything.

It is your smile that will light up the world and your laughter that will reclaim it from the depths of despair. These are your gifts my children, use them well and for the good of all.

Saturday August 26, 2006

Astrology is not spirit but it can sometimes convey spiritual messages. Conceivably anything that is aimed at one cannot be written in a way that also conveys its message to millions, at least not specific messages. No, it is not a con, just a tool, as are runes, cards, ribbons, numbers, etc. Spirit is infinite and plans everything. Your star sign, like your name, is pre-planned, pre-ordained. Thus as with numerology this has relevance but you cannot live your lives as to what you think is written in your star sign. It is your instincts that, as always, guide you. It is your instincts that make you interpret the message, your instincts that make you read them one day and not another. Your instincts are your soul; it is these that guide you.

You are born at the right time for you. That this corresponds to a certain time of year, month, day, and so on is, of course, pre-planned and pre-ordained. That there are similarities between those who are born at certain times is, of course, not a coincidence. We are at one with the planets and the universe. The moon has sway on the earth and the planets have sway on the planet also. We are all matter and as such are affected by the movements of the planets. So, to answer your question astrology is not nonsense any more than it is nonsense that the moon affects the tides or the moon affects our psychic abilities. The reason we are affected by the moon's cycles is not only that predominately we are water but also our abilities to be more sensitive at this time pick up more of the negativity from within the earth's atmosphere. This madness is just a result of increased sensitivity to negative influences that prevail on this planet.

Sunday August 27, 2006

Alzheimer's is a disease of the physical body and the mind which is, of course, part of the physical body. In this sense it does not affect the spiritual mind. Therefore it is possible to communicate with the spirit of the person who is so afflicted. This is a form of spirit talking to spirit and this is done on a psychic rather than a spiritual level in the usual sense of mediums talking to the spirit of those who have gone back to spirit. It is possible to train oneself to speak on this level to the spirit of the person so afflicted. However, your earthly world would no doubt object to someone purporting to speak for someone who is in this state. But, of course, proof could be forthcoming. But it would have to be proof from the person which could, of course, be proof that is coming from spirit of those who have gone to spirit. A dilemma I think! But proof is proof whence soever it comes and where soever it comes. Again, safeguards are necessary as to the genuineness of the medium and their authenticity to prevent exploitation of that person and their family. But it is always thus, and as always on the earth plane there are too many who are ready to abuse their gifts. An unavoidable part of your human existence. On a more positive note it would be a great leap forward for those with this condition to be able to communicate. As with all things within the earthly plane these ideas take time to ferment and take root and to gain acceptance.

It may be, of course, that they do not wish to communicate. Their spirit is perhaps enjoying the peace and tranquillity that this affords them. No, this is not flippancy, just an observation.

Thursday September 7, 2006

The eyes are truly the windows of the soul. Spirit is within all and recognition is there to remind you that you too are spirit. Your eyes too are the windows of your soul. What do people see when they look into your eyes? Do they see love, peace and light or do they see pain?

It is your choice what they see. Choose love, peace and light. Then truly will your spirit shine through and truly will you be recognised.

Thursday November 31, 2006

Life's journey is very much like a journey on a boat. The pace is leisurely until you reach the rapids then it speeds up and it becomes a challenge. As with the rapids you must make decisions quickly but never fear I am with you and will always be with you.

When the current is rough you have to make a little more effort to achieve the same things. But it is not the waves that can defeat you but your fellow sailors who at times seem intent on sinking the ship. It is at times like this when you need to remember that God is always on your side and only has your best interests at heart. It is just that his idea of your best interests and your idea of your best interests are often different. Your goal is to evolve and you will always do this even though you may think otherwise. It is not possible to evolve backwards so be cheerful and count your blessings not your troubles.

Thursday February 22, 2007

Symbols are often used by spirit to send messages to those of you that understand. If you see something that is significant in some way then it is possibly meant as a sign for you. Everybody has different signs because you are all individuals therefore what is important to one may not be to another.

If you need an answer to something ask for a sign and you will be given a sign. Who is to say what is relevant and what is irrelevant? You have chosen your life therefore it stands to reason that you will have chosen signs that are significant to you. Thus you will know what is relevant and what is irrelevant.

You must be careful in the use of signs. Too often a sign is expected to be of a deeper meaning. You may receive a small push from spirit from time to time, or an image is recognised as significant but you must also rely on your own free will and learn to trust your own judgement. Enjoy the birds or flowers or music you see round you. They are proof of the joys of life. Spirit can only share these joys briefly and must not be expected to guide your every step. However, once in a while a loved one can take the time to give you a remembrance link, but this is to show they care. Your choices should be your own—personal responsibility is one of the seven principles after all.

Symbols have always been used as ways of communicating because they transcend language.

The signs of religions distinguish between religions—the ones on your cover should unite religions. You are designing a new

145

symbol or sign that will transcend religious differences because it is all and it is none. Thus as spirituality transcends all religions thus will your sign do the same.

Footnote—This message was given to Julie Fell at the same time.

Bibliography

Brahma Kumaris World Spiritual University
www.brahmakumaris.org.uk

Feldman, Fred (1998). "Death." In E. Craig (Ed.), "Routledge Encyclopedia of Philosophy." London: Routledge. Retrieved July 24, 2006, from http://www.rep.routledge.com/article/ N011SECT2

"The Biology of Belief" by Dr Bruce Lipton

Garber, Daniel (1998, 2003). "Descartes, René." In E. Craig (Ed.), "Routledge Encyclopedia of Philosophy." London: Routledge. Retrieved July 24, 2006, from http://www.rep.routledge.com/ article/DA026SECT7

Frankfurt, H. "Equality as a moral idea." Reprinted in "Debates in Contemporary Political Philosophy—An Anthology 2003 The Open University": Routledge Taylor and Francis Group pp 82-97